Books by
WILLIAM TRUFANT FOSTER
AND
WADDILL CATCHINGS

. .
.

MONEY
PROFITS
BUSINESS WITHOUT A BUYER
THE ROAD TO PLENTY
PROGRESS AND PLENTY

————

POLLAK FOUNDATION FOR ECONOMIC
RESEARCH
NEWTON, MASSACHUSETTS, U.S.A.

PUBLICATIONS
OF THE POLLAK FOUNDATION FOR
ECONOMIC RESEARCH

NUMBER THIRTEEN
PROGRESS AND PLENTY

Progress and Plenty

Two-Minute Talks on the Economics of Prosperity

BY

WILLIAM TRUFANT FOSTER

AND

WADDILL CATCHINGS

BOSTON AND NEW YORK

HOUGHTON MIFFLIN COMPANY

The Riverside Press Cambridge

1930

The Riverside Press
CAMBRIDGE · MASSACHUSETTS
PRINTED IN THE U.S.A.

Preface

LINCOLN is said to have written, on the fly-leaf of a book which a persistent agent asked him to recommend: 'For any one who likes this kind of book, it is a good book for him to read.' That is about all we can say for *Progress and Plenty*. No reader will like it who is prepared to give hours of sustained attention to economic theories. For this book is neither systematic nor comprehensive, neither technical nor thorough. It gives only one page to each topic. It omits altogether about six hundred pages of footnotes, with the references, definitions, qualifications, and exceptions which exacting scholars would and should require.

Our only defense is that these Two-Minute Talks were not written for exacting scholars. They were written for about three million readers of daily newspapers. And most of these readers — believe it or not — either get their economics in two-minute instalments, or do not get it at all.

The articles in this book were distributed by the McClure Newspaper Syndicate in 1929 and 1930, and were published in daily papers from Boston to Tokyo. They are among the measures taken by the Pollak Foundation to carry out its purpose. That purpose is 'to study the means whereby the economic activities of the world may be so directed, and the products so distributed, as to yield to the people generally the largest possible satisfactions.'

It is a sorry thought that some of these articles, resisting every effort to make them readable, serve only to sustain the reputation of economics as 'the dismal science.' Even so, they are not so dull as they would have been without the sprightly editorial touch of Constance Kent.

Contents

Contents

Contents

Contents

Contents

Contents

Contents

Contents

PROGRESS AND PLENTY

Progress and Plenty

BUSINESS prosperity breeds business depression. Whenever times get better, experience warns us that they are about to get worse. Why? Why can we not consolidate our gains?

And why must so many workers suffer from want of wealth, while the science of creating wealth advances with giant strides?

Aroused by these questions half a century ago, Henry George stirred the world with his impassioned *Progress and Poverty*. His solution of the problem proved unconvincing. The problem persists.

Why can we not have Progress and Plenty?

In seeking an answer, we may well start with the fact that unemployment in recent years has not been caused by war, or crop failures, or money panics, or the collapse of inflation, or lack of capital. The major permanent cause has been the increased output per worker, which has resulted from the use of new knowledge.

That cause of unemployment will continue. As it has thrown men out of work in the making of tires, shoes, and textiles, in pig-iron casting, flour milling, and meat packing, so it will throw more men out of work in more industries. Nobody knows where the blessing of increased knowledge will next bring the curse of decreased employment.

That curse is an indictment of the present order. To that extent, at least, Henry George was right. No system should be tolerated, unchanged, which applies new knowledge only at the tragic cost of human suffering — the suffering of the very millions who are least able to bear it.

Fortunately, this problem of unemployment — call it 'technological' or what you will — can be solved. Plainly, the inventive faculty which puts men out of work in old industries has ingenuity enough to put them to work in new industries.

3

Victims of Progress

WHAT has happened to the many thousands who have been displaced in our factories by machinery?

'The answer is simple,' says one of our Federal bureaus. 'They have gone into non-manufacturing pursuits.' But to the crowds that scan our dwindling columns of help-wanted 'ads' and besiege our employment offices in winters of depression, the answer does not seem so simple. Nor does it seem so simple to the taxicab drivers, manicurists, real estate agents, bond salesmen, and many others who are counted among the employed, though they have merely crowded their way, as a last resort, into vocations that were already overcrowded. There are many Victims of Progress.

Now comes news of the invention of a shoe machine that may throw another 10,000 factory hands out of work! Also a dispatch about a means of setting type simultaneously in many cities. But such news is no longer news. In countless industries, science has increased the productivity of labor.

And thrown many laborers out of work.

How many, nobody knows. We all know, however, that some 50,000 harvesting machines have taken the place of more than 100,000 farm laborers. We know that, in ten years, air control of New York subway train doors cut down the number of guards about 25 per cent, while the number of passengers increased about 50 per cent. We know, too, that Class I railroads greatly increased their business, and at the same time reduced the numbers on their payrolls by 13 per cent. Turning to manufacturing as a whole, we find that for every 100 workers employed in 1923, not more than 88 are employed to-day.

Ways must be devised of using the labor of men who are displaced by machines. There should be less waste of productive power. There should be fewer Victims of Progress.

No Problem?

EVERYBODY knows that this country actually does turn out at times far more goods than it is able to sell — not merely more hats, or cereals, or tires, or dresses that are too short or too long, but more goods in general. Consequently, every now and then, industry is obliged to curtail operations until, in the course of a painful year or two, the surplus stocks are sold at a loss.

Many business men, having admitted all this — in fact, having bitterly complained of all this — still hold to the old automatic-production-consumption theory. They contend that there really is no problem of consumer income; at least no problem with which Government or Industry may properly be concerned.

No problem? When wages are reduced seven billion dollars in a single year, while industry stagnates for want of the driving force of wages spent?

No problem? When warehouses are bulging with raw materials and men are thrown out of work, and factories are shut down, at the very time when countless people are in want of the goods which millions of willing workers are not allowed to make out of these surplus materials?

No problem? When producers are constantly afraid that they will produce too much, and consumers that they cannot get enough?

No problem? When President Hoover declares that we have 'an equipment and skill in production that yield us a surplus of commodities for export beyond any compensation we can usefully take by way of imported commodities'; a surplus, in other words, made by our own workers, which they can neither buy at home nor exchange for consumables from abroad?

Wage-earners, at least, are sure that such a problem exists! To them it is as real and insistent as the grocery bill.

5

Better Still

THE Leviathan is steaming at the dock. It is a mechanical wonder. It can carry across the ocean in a week more goods than the fleet of Columbus could have carried in a generation. We can trust the engineering machinery to do its part, with friction reduced to a minimum.

Will the Leviathan, then, fulfill its purpose? Will it carry abroad a full cargo, and bring back a full cargo in exchange? Probably not. We cannot trust our economic machinery to do its part. There is too much friction: too much of the sand of politics is thrown into the gears.

And here are huge banks, bristling with mechanical contrivances; computing machines, telephones, automatic alarms. Here are vaults piled high with money; money, invented by man for his own convenience; a marvelous device for facilitating the production and exchange of goods.

What do we do with all this mechanically-perfect equipment? Do we operate it steadily, so that, day in and day out, it performs its part in the world's work? Do we maintain a circuit flow of money that keeps our factories busy and our labor employed?

Far from it. Every now and then, we allow the channels to become clogged. We fail to provide consumers with enough money to move the vast stocks of goods which our mechanical ingenuity has piled up. Then prices tumble; orders are canceled; furnaces are banked; and again the unemployed tramp the streets in larger numbers.

Ships are ready. Mills are ready. Machines are ready. Materials are ready. Marvelous technical equipment! If we only knew how to keep it running, we could feed and clothe and house twice our population.

Or, better still, rescue from poverty virtually every person in our present population who is willing to work.

6

Are We Economic Illiterates?

W E are a nation of economic illiterates. At least, so says
one of our bank presidents.

Well, what of it? Are we not a nation of scientific illiterates
as well? Do we know more about the principles of physics than
we know about the principles of banking? Does the man in the
street know more about hydraulic pumps than he knows about
marginal utility; or more about the effect of electrolysis on
chemical compounds than he knows about the effect of tariffs
on the cost of living?

Probably not. But scientific problems do not confound us.
We turn them over to experts. We do not take a vote on how to
purify our water supply, or how to construct a tunnel. We do
not care how many people believe, and how many people do not
believe, that an antitoxin will destroy the germs of diphtheria.
We try it on the germs in the laboratory and deal with the
disease accordingly. On such subjects, we know that one man's
opinion is as good as another's, and neither is worth anything.

Economic problems, on the other hand, we try to settle by
popular vote. Everybody is supposed to know how to draw up
tariff schedules and regulate railroad rates. Everybody, by
a kind of intuition, is expected to tell a good monetary system
from a bad one. Everybody is supposed to know how to solve
'the farm problem'; and a few, at least, are supposed to know
what the problem is. Such matters we do not refer to experts.
We settle them by taking votes.

That is why it does not matter, for practical purposes, what
the voters know about the law of falling bodies, but does matter
a good deal what they know about the law of falling prices.
That is why economic illiteracy is far more serious than scientific illiteracy.

7

Why Not Double Our Output?

WHY is it that we cannot buy more with our wages? Mainly because we do not create more.

Why this failure to create? One fact is clear: the trouble is not lack of capacity. That was proved during the War. Even with millions of able-bodied men taken from productive effort, the workers who were left produced so much that they not only supplied the wealth that was sunk at sea and blown up in battle, not only supplied the Army and Navy and peoples abroad, but produced enough more to enable the people at home to enjoy as high a standard of living as before the War.

Every day we read of new inventions and new sources of power that, if used, would unbelievably increase the productivity of labor. By the mere turning of a switch we now command a hundred times more energy than all the man-power and all the horse-power of our grandfathers' time.

The fact that incapacity to produce is not the trouble is also shown by the heights we have reached in time of peace. If business could keep on gaining at the rate even of our moderately good years, far higher standards of living would be certain. Proved capacity, moreover, is far below potential capacity. The engineering societies, under the direction of Herbert Hoover, have shown that we are equipped to double our production.

To double the output of everything — of matches and motion pictures and medicines, and every other commodity — is neither possible nor desirable; but to double the output of things in general, with the proportions determined, as they are now determined, by the free choices of the people, is both possible and desirable.

Such gains would be no more than enough to provide all of us with comfort, health, security, and education. Any lower aim is indefensible.

'Laudable Pus'

ONCE upon a time surgeons looked eagerly, following an operation, for the appearance of pus in the wound. It was known as 'laudable pus.' It was regarded as a good sign. The patient, supposedly, had to get worse before he could get better — if he got better. Healing by 'first intention' — the clean, quick drawing together of tissues — occurred so infrequently as to be considered miraculous. Germs, to be sure, were treated as undesirable aliens, but no attempt was made to reduce the quota admitted.

Then an English surgeon advanced an astounding theory. It was not enough, he said, to fight the destroyers after they were in. They should not even be among those present at surgical operations. To-day a surgeon who spoke of 'laudable pus' would be ridiculed out of his profession.

But how complacently we still regard the sore spots of the profession of business! We still talk about 'the usual volume of unemployment' as surgeons used to talk about 'the usual amount of pus.' When more men lose their jobs, we talk as though business, necessarily, were getting worse in order that it might get better.

We calmly accept the picturesque contrast between the man sitting luxuriously in the chauffeur-driven car, flashing through the wintry park, and the shivering derelict, huddled on the park bench. Light and shade. Hard on the shade, of course, but a necessary part of the picture.

'Laudable pus!'

Our appreciation for that sort of ugly realism is falling off. Poverty is ugly. It is an open sore. It is not laudable. And it is not necessary. That is equally true of a large part of the unemployment that comes in cycles. Economic wounds need not get worse before they get better. They can be healed by 'first intention.'

9

Making Friends With Your Luck

TO make friends with your luck is the part of wisdom — but only if there is nothing else you can do about it.

To *make* the best of outrageous conditions is a false virtue. To *get* the best of them is a real virtue.

In short, patience is a virtue only up to the point where it becomes a crime.

Back in 1800, for a man to grit his teeth and endure repeated attacks of appendicitis was heroic. Now it is idiotic.

Back in 1800, the family doctor shrugged his shoulders and said, 'What can't be cured, must be endured.'

But happily there were other men who said, 'What can't be endured, must be cured.' They discovered anesthetics.

In economics, also, progress is born of revolt, not resignation.

'I accept the universe,' said Margaret Fuller.

'Gad, she'd better!' replied Thomas Carlyle.

But Carlyle was the last man meekly to accept conditions in that part of the universe in which he lived.

Back in 1800, some of the economists accepted universal poverty — for the workers. 'The great masses of wage-earners,' said these dismal theorists, 'never can rise far above the lowest level of subsistence. They must make friends with their luck.'

But there were heretical economists, even in those dark days. That sort of luck, they insisted, was no friend of a wage-earner; it wasn't even a desirable acquaintance.

Now, business men as well as economists agree with the daring dissenters of a century ago. They insist that wage-earners can and should rise far above even the highest level of subsistence which they have yet reached; that real wages have never been high enough.

It is safe for wage-earners to shake hands with their luck, when it carries credentials like that.

Sing-Side Seat Philosophers

NOT long ago, a pleasant French gentleman, by the name of Coué, visited our shores. No just settlement of the French debt can be made without taking into account what he did to us. Departing, he left behind a trail of criminal dependence on the efficacy of a catchy couplet:

'Every day, in every way, everything is getting better and better.'

Lulled by this lush assurance, addicts of the theory sit contentedly in their sing-side seats, and watch the world improve.

And it does improve. Make no mistake about that.

But what makes it improve? Certainly not crooning couplets. Certainly not the mere rolling on of days.

Time, left to its own resources, produces nothing but antiques; and not enough of them to supply the demand.

Assuring each other that everything is all right, doesn't make it all right.

It may produce a Mr. Micawber.

It cannot produce a Mr. Ford.

It may bring contentment to the employer who says: 'There is only the usual amount of unemployment. Why worry?'

It cannot bring any comfort at all to the employer who has sense enough to know that 'the usual amount of unemployment' is a national disgrace.

It may be reassuring to those who emphasize the fact that the labor of machines is fast replacing the back-breaking toil of human beings.

It is less reassuring to those human beings for whom a blue slip — in the pay envelope — emphasizes the fact that *they* have been replaced.

The cold fact is that nothing is getting better, any day, in any way, anywhere, except as some human being is making it better.

'Funny Feelings'

DAVID BERNSTEIN walked into a New York police station and confessed that he pushed James Tucker off a Brooklyn elevated platform. Bernstein, father of four children, said he had been out of work for two years, and this had preyed on his mind. He got 'funny feelings' and 'went crazy.' Four children, even with plenty of money, are a problem. Four children, with no money, explain plenty of 'funny feelings.'

Then there was the case of Patricia Bennett, a pretty little New York City girl who ran away from home in search of a job. She found one. Arraigned before Judge Mulqueen, she found also that her job — which consisted of holding up a man and robbing him of seven dollars — might cost her fifteen years in jail. Patricia wept. She had been a silly girl.

But what shall we say of Helen Dorf, a widow who appeared in court the same day, in the same city, charged with throwing herself in front of an on-coming subway express train? She had lost her job, she explained. She had hunted in vain for another. In despair, she decided that her two children would be better off if she killed herself. The Judge, learning that the dejected mother was perfectly able and willing to work, promptly found her a good place to work.

Was she, too, a silly girl? Or is it more to the point to say that she lives in a silly world — a world in which at least one competent widow finds no means of supporting her children until she jumps in front of a subway express?

Perhaps the State should have taken these three desperate citizens in hand sooner; at the time, let us say, when the 'funny feelings' caused by unemployment first assailed them.

At that time, with an adequate system of employment exchanges, it would have cost little to administer first aid. Nothing elaborate, of course; merely some simple violence preventative like — well, for instance, a job.

'Advice to Uplifters'

UNDER this caption a Southern newspaper says: 'If all humanitarians were put on a six weeks' diet of their own creed, the world would be vastly better off. First, it would free us of a woeful amount of meddling; and, second, it would convince the uplifters themselves that their panaceas — education, higher wages, equality of wealth, or whatever they advocate — will not cure our social ills and turn us into an Arcadian dream.'

This reminds us of the tramp who beat a rug in return for his breakfast. When he brought in the rug, the owner pointed out several holes. 'These holes weren't there when I gave you this rug,' she said, accusingly.

The tramp eyed her reproachfully. 'Lady,' he asked, 'if they weren't there, where were they?'

Perhaps the cures for our social ills do not lie in education, higher wages, and a more equitable distribution of wealth. But if they aren't there, where are they?

Or should we assume that there are *no* cures for social ills? That we must go on to the end, patiently enduring poverty and all its heartaches?

The other day, in Boston, a young man offered himself for sale for $2500. A boyish gesture, of course; but, after all, he was confronted with starvation or the humiliation of being fed by charity. Wouldn't the wages urged by meddling 'uplifters' — not *higher* wages, but *any* wages — mean something to him?

Uplifters are a meddlesome lot, no doubt. They are often tiresome. Often, too, they are stupidly ineffectual. But they have one grace which covers a multitude of stupidities. They are never light-hearted about other people's troubles. They may not succeed in transforming life, for all of us, into an Arcadian dream; but to their everlasting credit, they are not reconciled to its remaining, for any of us, a Stygian nightmare.

13

Crashing the Gates

SMALL boys, crashing the gates at a football game, were promptly seized and locked up in a steel cage, ungilded but stout, under the Harvard stadium. They were permitted to peer out through the bars — but not at the game. Bostonians sat up and took shocked notice. The Welfare Society rushed over to see what all the shouting was about, and did a little shouting of its own.

Said its officers: 'Children are entitled to more consideration than grown-ups.'

About the same time, an Italian woman was tried in Boston for shooting her husband, and found guilty. The jury, who heard that 'she had borne the man's abuse for years, but couldn't stand seeing her children tortured,' brought in a light verdict.

Bostonians, devoted as they are to Harvard and to law, are also, it seems, in their quaint way, devoted to children. So are all the rest of us. Men without jobs we can dismiss from our minds. 'The usual amount of unemployment,' we say, and feel vaguely comforted. But children without food we cannot dismiss from our hearts. We have not sunk to easy announcements about the 'usual amount of child suffering.'

Millions of men who want to work tramp doggedly up and down our 'Stupidity Streets,' looking for jobs that aren't there. We are sorry, but what can we do?

Much, perhaps, if we stop to think that back of these millions of men are millions of children — children shut up in cages of deprivation, peering out wistfully at a world that should be full of joy. Shut up in cages because their fathers are unable to crash the gates of a job.

'We are sorry, but what can —' No, that formula may do for men, 'but children are entitled to more consideration than grown-ups.' Being sorry for them is not enough.

Other People's Children

'THE saddest fact,' says *Hygeia*, 'is that heart-disease, which now heads our list of death-causes, attacks children, particularly children under ten. Most childhood cases originate in damp, gloomy homes, under poor living conditions.'

This, very likely, describes an entirely different home from your home. Still, reading the item leaves you with a queer feeling. Try as you will, you can't banish it. There's a solidarity among parents that no discrepancy in bank balances quite dissolves.

When a little girl is kidnapped, it is always, for one horrible moment, *your* little girl. When a prematurely business-like voice shrills, 'Paper, mister,' it is, for a startled second, *your* boy's voice. Your boy's voice, happily, hasn't any anxious note in it. You see to that. Nor does your boy ever shiver at the impact of bleak winds on thinly-clad shoulders. 'Junior' is at home, you remind yourself, warm and fed.

Nevertheless, you can't put out of your mind the child who contracts heart disease in a damp, gloomy house. It isn't really Junior or his baby sister, but it might be.

More than a million wage-earning fathers in this country feel the same way about their Juniors and their baby girls, but are helpless to give them what all children need. These fathers are employed, it is true; but their pay of twenty-two dollars a week, or less, must feed, clothe, and shelter four or more members of the family. That accounts for a lot of damp, gloomy surroundings.

What can *you* do about it? The first thing you can do is to admit to yourself that the problem of poverty, with all its damp, gloomy fixings, is *your* problem. Once you have accepted this responsibility, you will do *something*.

It is not easy to dismiss another father's poverty when you say: 'This father's poverty, as long as it exists, is *my* poverty.'

'The Menace of Materialism'

FOR centuries men have praised the virtues of the poor. The poor do have virtues, many of them: tolerance, sympathy, often an amazing generosity to those even poorer than themselves. But these are the virtues of the poor. They are not the virtues of poverty.

Poverty has no virtues. It has not even the virtue, so long and persistently ascribed to it, of developing the 'spirituality' of its victims. Well-meaning souls, bent on making the best of a condition that has no best, have assured us that poverty, under its ugly disguise, is a heavenly disciplinarian. Released from poverty, it is said, the great masses of the poor would relapse into gross materialism.

This doctrine seems to be preached most eloquently by people who are comfortably well off. We conclude that they themselves have developed spirituality without the beneficial influence of poverty. But if *they* can escape materialism, why not all of us?

Now comes Henry Ford with the assertion that poverty is not an evangel at all. It fosters, he says, not spirituality but materialism. The unfortunate man whose mind is continually bent to the problem of his next meal or his next night's shelter is a materialist perforce. How shall this unfortunate man be rescued?

By prayer and fasting?

'No,' says Mr. Ford. 'This man cannot get his mind off the grindstone of material needs. But emancipate him by economic security and the appurtenances of social decency and comfort, and instead of making him more of a materialist, you liberate him from the menace of materialism.'

Mr. Ford is a practical man. When he says, 'Emancipate this man by economic security,' he is not talking of Utopia. He is talking of something that can be done, 'now, at this time.'

'Smothered in Material Comfort'

WE are smothered in material comfort,' says Katharine Gerould, 'and we do not know enough to look for comfort of a different kind. Only aristocrats can make a spiritual use of leisure. The man who has fought all his life for enough bread to keep him and his family alive will always give undue emphasis to bread. Only in the next generation, probably, will he turn to the things of the mind: knowledge, taste, delicate experience. The people who know what money is good for are those who have had it long enough to learn.'

This sounds like the famous remark of Patrick McDuff: 'New shoes are so stiff, I can't get 'em on till I've worn 'em a few times.' How can anybody wear prosperity gracefully and without squeaks until he has tried it awhile? The Butterscotchman, told that he would have to run in order to get warm, replied bitterly that he would have to get warm before he *could* run.

Nobody can learn to spend either money or leisure wisely, except by having a little to spend. No darling daughter can learn to swim who hangs her clothes on a hickory limb and doesn't go near the water. 'The next generation' is too far away. All of us ought to be 'smothered in material comfort' right here and now. Never fear — comfortable critics — we shall recover our breaths, presently, just as you did. We, too, shall acquire an appreciation for knowledge, taste, and delicate experience.

Jesus, above all others, inspired men to look for comfort of another kind. Laying up treasures on earth was not the gist of His gospel. Yet He once paused in His teaching, not to make sure that His listeners were 'aristocrats' with a cultural background which would enable them to turn to things of the spirit. He paused to make sure that they were amply supplied with the 'material comfort' of loaves and fishes.

Want and Wants

THERE are two ways to reach satisfaction. One way is to get what you want. The other way is not to want it.

The Puritans believed that it was godly not to want things — that is, things which added to human comfort or pleasure. They objected to bear-baiting, says Macaulay, not so much because it gave pain to the bears, as because it gave pleasure to the spectators.

This concept of the virtue of 'doing without' still gets in our way. Most of us, it is true, don't do without much more than we *have* to, but we have a sneaking idea that we *ought* to.

The new economics declares otherwise. Pruning our wants, it tells us, is not necessarily an economic virtue. Indeed, in so far as such self-denial brings hardship on others as well as on ourselves, the practice is not even spiritually sound.

We used to suppose that there was just so much wealth in the world, and the fewer things we grasped for ourselves, the more were left for others. But it doesn't always work out that way.

The more goods we want and make it our business to get, the more goods will be made. The more making of goods, the more jobs. And a job for every one who wants a job is one of the chief goals of organized society.

The more we get of the goods which really add to our health, usefulness, and pleasure, the better off we are. There is not so wide a chasm as the Puritans thought there was between 'goods' and 'good.' On the contrary, a dearth of this world's goods — poverty — is the cause of much of this world's disease, ill-temper, and crime.

Blessed is that consumer who is weighed by merchants and found wanting. Satisfied customers may be our best advertisement; but customers with unsatisfied wants, and the will and the money to satisfy these wants, are our best employment agencies.

Can You Answer This Letter?

NOT long ago, we received this letter:

Dear Sirs:

When Wu Koshung was visiting New York City, he was taken down town on subway trains. At Ninety-Sixth Street he was rushed out of the local train and jammed into an express train. At Forty-Second Street he was rushed from the express train, and jammed into a local train.

'Just think!' said his host. 'By using the express train part of the way we have saved five minutes.'

'But what,' asked Wu Koshung, 'will you do with the extra five minutes?'

As far as this serene Chinese official could see, Americans already had more time than they knew how to spend wisely.

Well, what has this to do with economics? A lot. You are always calling for more wages in order that people can buy more things, in order to stimulate business to turn out still more things. But already wage-earners have more things than they know how to use wisely — more wages than they know how to spend wisely. What would they do with an extra five dollars a week? Man does not live by bread alone. He has an immortal soul. Have you ever thought of that?

Yours truly,
JAMES R. BRENNARD

Yes, Mr. Brennard, we *have* thought of that. But we shall not try to answer your question. We, also, are able to buy all the things we really need. Allow us to refer you to a man who knows far more about this subject than we do. Pick him out at random from among the ten million wage-earners who are receiving less than forty dollars a week. Ask *him* if he could possibly spend an extra five dollars a week on things — yes, on things — without losing his immortal soul.

'Free Facilities for Fasting'

WE have received an invitation, addressed to the 'Illuminati,' whoever they are, to join the World-Wide Fasting Movement. The invitation is signed by Dr. Aron, Ph.D., A.M., Secretary of the Fasting Clubs of Chicago. One aim of these clubs, it is announced, is to provide 'Free Facilities for Fasting.'

In order to attain spiritual exaltation, we are advised to join the Fasters on a private estate in the Rocky Mountains, there to experience 'The Ideal Fast,' lasting forty days. As a special inducement, we are assured of an opportunity to meet Fasting's Three Daughters: Physical Elimination, Mental Concentration, and Spiritual Illumination.

Fasting, we are told, will solve the economic problem, increase industrial efficiency 1,000 per cent, and reveal the straight road to love. If that is not enough to convert you, read on. Fasting 'crushes the world-wide inferiority complex!' Among those quoted in proof are Dante, Dr. Aron, and Moses.

Now, are you convinced? Well, to tell the truth, neither are we. As far as we can see, an abundance of free facilities for fasting in Armenia and China has not yet solved their economic problems. Nor are we sure that the industries which have provided their employees with most frequent opportunities for fasting have increased their efficiency. And for crushing an inferiority complex, we know nothing quite so effective as a steady job at good wages — wages that guarantee good food, and plenty of it, for the whole family.

No, Dr. Aron, a private estate in the Rocky Mountains is hardly the place to investigate this subject. Try our plan. Visit any mill town or mining town where fathers have been out of work forty days — not an 'ideal' forty days, but the usual kind. Stroll down any street where the workers live. See for yourself the spiritual exaltation that comes from fasting.

A Chinese View of Business

SAYS Kiang Kang-Hu, in *The Nation's Business*, 'To us Chinese scholars, to be busy is distasteful. I can never understand the American business man's life. Every one is busy every moment. It amuses me. But, thanks be to God, I myself am not in the center of it. I am like one who visits a tragic-comic play. I can enjoy it so much, simply because I take no part in it.'

On the other hand, the American business man, observing epidemic and starvation among millions of Chinese, is not at all like one who visits a tragic-comic play. To him, such suffering is stark tragedy. And he cannot enjoy it by taking no part in it. His humanitarian impulses *force* him to take part in it.

That is why, time and time again, American business men have poured into China, for relief of plague and famine, millions of dollars' worth of the material necessities of life — material necessities which were created by the 'tragic-comic' activities of busy American men.

To these men, some things are even more distasteful than being busy. One of these is the poverty which four thousand years of the Chinese philosophy of life have failed to conquer.

Yet Kiang Kang-Hu comes to the United States to tell us that American business men 'are life-long slaves of their material desires.' Has he not observed, in his own country, millions of men who are life-long slaves of their material poverty?

Which is worse? The American business man knows which is worse, but he chooses neither. By means of the creation of wealth, he is gradually escaping both the bondage of materialism and the bondage of poverty. That, to be sure, is keeping him busy, though not so many hours a day as formerly.

It is the man facing starvation who has no escape from the slavery of his material desires. He is of necessity a materialist.

Mass Production for Europe?

SHOULD Europe Americanize its methods of production? 'There is,' says André Siegfried, author of *America Comes of Age*, 'no problem of greater moment.'

The first step in clarifying this problem is to forget that mass production originated in America. Progress has no nationality. If mass production is progress, it will make a non-stop flight across the Atlantic, and make itself at home in Europe without benefit of passports.

The way to decide whether mass production really is progress is to examine its fruits. The main fruits in the United States are longer jobs, higher real wages, and higher standards of living.

But Mr. Siegfried evidently fears that Americans may become 'thing-minded'; that as individuals they may become spiritually submerged; smothered by the avalanche of goods which they produce.

'America,' he says, 'has emphasized the prestige of production. Rightly or wrongly, we fear that the individual, considered not as a producer or as a consumer, but as a human being, may appear in the long run to be the loser.'

It may be possible, as a mental exercise, to consider the individual, not as a producer or as a consumer, but as a human being. When this is tried in real life, however, the 'individual' is out of luck. To be a human being, it is necessary to be a consumer; and American consumers have never found their idealism blighted by the assurance of three square meals a day. Idealism persists not on undernourishment, but in spite of it.

The best centers for developing individuality are well-nurtured, well-housed, and well-clothed, in short, self-respecting human beings. Mass production in America has greatly increased the proportion of such human beings. Its goal must be to make any other kind of human being unknown.

Alice-in-Wonderland Economics

ALICE–IN–WONDERLAND had to run fast in order to stay where she was. We run fast every day in a Wonderland of Business which has greater mysteries than that.

Sometimes we produce so much that the only way to keep industry going seems to be to dump goods into the sea, or give them away, or sell them to people who are unable to pay for them. We succeed, by strenuous efforts, in sending more and more of our own real wealth abroad; but we always contrive to prevent other nations from sending as much real wealth to us. While our factories are running part-time because consumers are not buying enough, we blame consumers for extravagant buying. Then, when industry wanes because it lacks consumers, we put taxes on consumption. And precisely when business needs the stimulus of wages spent, we reduce wages.

Alice-in-Wonderland found nothing stranger than all this!

Is it not possible to prevent these setbacks? To shorten and smooth out these detours on 'The Road to Plenty'?

'Not under the established economic order.' That is one point upon which conservatives and revolutionists agree. The *conservatives* insist that as long as men are free to produce what they please, and consumers are free to buy what they please, and as long as business is subject to all the caprices of women and weather, just so long will there be periods of excessive unemployment. Wherefore, we should be content.

As long, insist the *revolutionists*, as both production and consumption are restricted by a profit-seeking, money-monopolizing, rent-and-interest-charging system, just so long will society be cursed with underconsumption and resultant unemployment. Wherefore, we should overthrow the whole system.

But more and more thinkers are coming to believe that our chief economic problem *can* be solved, and solved without a revolution.

Fifty Years Ago

FIFTY years ago Thomas A. Edison invented the incandescent light. A grateful nation is celebrating.

Orators in ten thousand schools are trying in vain to add to the fame of the inventor — trying in vain to exaggerate the blessings of his invention — trying in vain to explain to children who were born in this age of electricity, what life was like without it.

What has happened to industry in the last half century is beyond the imagination of these children. Thanks to Edison and the researches of men inspired by him, an unknown something now flows, in some unknown way, precisely where man wants it to flow. And behold, age-old burdens are lifted from the backs of those who labor and are heavy laden.

At this moment a single workman, sitting in a clean, quiet room before an instrument board, reaches out his arm, turns a few small switches, and makes Niagara Falls illuminate a hundred cities and run the wheels of a thousand factories.

The average American workman to-day has, in effect, a hundred slaves working for him incessantly. He has a large measure of freedom from human slavery, achieved by enslaving the forces of nature.

Rightly we rejoice. Rightly we honor the inventor of the incandescent light.

But we can honor him with something better than commemorative exercises.

A thousand Niagara Falls, or the equivalent in power, are still running to waste. A thousand potential power stations lie hidden in the bowels of the earth. A hundred thousand willing workers have no work to do.

Still, there are a million farmers and their wives and children who have not yet achieved the luxury of a single incandescent light.

'Nice People'

NOBODY knows who issued the dictum, 'Nice People don't talk about money.' Some wife, it may be, who couldn't balance her accounts to her husband's satisfaction; or some husband, horrified by his wife's appeal for a cash allowance. Anyway, some one said it, and many people believe it. Yet, admit it or not, there is nothing of such importance as money to so many human beings so many hours of every day.

To get around the taboo against money as a topic of polite conversation, 'Nice People' hit on a clever device. They simply amassed the money, and let it do the talking for them. That was an admirable solution, except for the people who couldn't amass money. They, perforce, kept right on talking about it.

This hypocrisy was too much for Emerson. 'Do not gloze and prate and mystify,' he wrote in his Journal. 'Here our dear, grand Alcott says: "You shall dig in my field for a day and I will give you a dollar for it, but it shall not be a business transaction!" It makes me sick. Whilst money is the measure really adopted by us all as the most convenient of all material values, let us not affectedly disuse the name and mystify ourselves and others.'

Emerson, manifestly, was not a 'nice' person. He not only openly called a dollar a dollar, but sometimes figured on how much he could contrive to buy with one.

Surely the great philosopher would have rejoiced to see our day; for in our day money can be discussed. We not only talk openly about money; we declare that no family should be without it. Yet no thunderbolt of social wrath falls on our heads.

The flow of conversation need no longer cease abruptly at the mention of money. It should expand into serious discussion about the flow of money, and consideration of better means for controlling the flow.

Why Not Abolish Money?

BOSWELL tells us that the great Doctor Johnson was once embarrassed. A doting mother expected him to praise a piece played by her daughter. But the gruff doctor was silent. 'Do you realize,' asked the mother, 'how difficult that composition is?'

'Difficult!' exclaimed Doctor Johnson. 'Difficult! Would to God it were impossible.'

To-day some people who are expected to praise the complicated economic machinery, which every now and then throws a million men out of work, wish that the whole difficult achievement had been impossible. And since money is at the foundation of it, they want to abolish money.

But how could there be a nation without money? Imagine the Treasury Department trying to collect, from four million taxpayers, a billion dollars of taxes in the form of goods — strawberries, short stories, pig-iron, legal opinions, theater tickets, cut flowers, and so forth. Imagine trying to transport all these tax payments, in just the right amounts, at just the right times, to pay the wages of Government clerks in Washington, teachers in Alaska, contractors in New Orleans, soldiers in the Philippines. That task would not only be difficult: it would be impossible!

As a matter of fact, the whole industrial world has become so dependent on money that to millions of people the sudden destruction of money would mean death by starvation.

The success of men is reckoned most commonly, and their efforts rewarded, in salaries and wages. Human ambitions and activities tend to gravitate around money.

Mechanics measures an engine in terms of horse power; dietetics measures an egg in terms of calories; but economics measures both engines and eggs in terms of dollars. In fact, without such a measure there would be no science of economics.

Why Not Trade by Barter?

LIEUTENANT CAMERON gives this account of his difficulties in buying a boat from natives in Africa: 'Syde's agent wished to be paid in ivory, of which I had none; but I found that Mohammed Ibn Salib had ivory and wanted cloth. Still, as I had no cloth, this did not assist me greatly until I heard that Mohammed Ibn Gharib had cloth and wanted wire. This I fortunately possessed. So I gave Ibn Gharib the requisite amount of wire; whereupon he handed over cloth to Ibn Salib, who in his turn gave Syde's agent the wished-for ivory. Then he allowed me to have the boat.'

That case illustrates the inconvenience of trade by barter.

In this country to-day are the makers of ten thousand different things — windmills, coffins, calcium lights, wooden legs, steam rollers, jew's-harps, and all the rest. Suppose each worker were paid, as workers were once paid, in shares of the products of his own labor. What a job he would have lugging them around with him, and trying to use them in place of money, in his daily trading with the butcher, the baker, and the candle-stick maker!

In the shoe factory there is a bookkeeper, and a sales manager, and a cutter, and a finisher, and a night-watchman; and no one of them produces anything which he can offer to the baker in exchange for bread. The baker does not want their products or their services, any more than he wants the poet's masterpiece. Neither does the poet want his pay in overalls, nor the jeweler's office boy his pay in wedding rings. The only way to satisfy everybody is by means of an interposed something which everybody knows that everybody else will accept in exchange for whatever he has to sell.

A society in which a trader has to seek a wire-cloth-ivory-boat chain of exchanges could not possibly become the specialized industrial society of to-day.

Why Not Use Cows for Money?

MEN have not always used gold and paper money as a medium of exchange. Once they used cows. In fact, our word 'pecuniary' comes from the Latin word which means cattle. It is said that many other things have been used as money: among them, tobacco, bullets, shells, furs, and dried fish. In the struggle for existence, the fittest survived.

It is easy to see why cows did not survive as currency. Even the Greeks, who expressed the value of a coat of armor in terms of cows, must have discovered that cows, however admirable for some purposes, are not entirely satisfactory as a medium of exchange. They are not easy for ladies to take along when shopping. Nor are they divisible in making change, at least not without trouble to the traders, and damage to the cows. Nor are they durable: they have a way of dying. Worse still, no two cows are of exactly the same value. That is why cows are not required to do the work performed by money — 'the pale and common drudge 'tween man and man.'

There is still another attribute of money that helps to explain how gold survived. It is easy to recognize gold. It is easy, for that matter, to recognize a cow; but an acceptable currency must satisfy *all* the tests, and no commodity possesses all the essential qualities in so high a degree as gold. No other commodity, meeting the other tests, is so easily carried about as gold. No other commodity, equally good in other respects, is both infinitely divisible and virtually indestructible. If a gold coin had been placed in circulation in the boyhood days of Methuselah, and had since been subjected only to the ordinary uses of currency, it would still be a gold coin.

The textbooks use big words to sum up all this. They say nothing makes a good medium of exchange unless it has portability, divisibility, durability, uniformity, and cognizability.

Is Money a Standard of Value?

WHEN you visit Washington, go to the Bureau of Standards and take a look at the 'standard yard.' It is kept, at uniform temperature, in a glass case. You will have to view it through a telescope. You will not be allowed to go near it, lest the heat of your body change the length of the bar one ten-thousandth part of an inch.

How ridiculous it would be to use, in place of this standard yard, the waist measurement of the President of the United States. How the 'standard' would have changed from Taft to Wilson, and from Coolidge to Hoover! Yet, at one time, the yard actually did vary with the girths of the chieftains.

Even now, the so-called money 'standards' of the world vary far more than that — more than the belt measures of the Fat Lady and the Living Skeleton at the circus. That is why we use index numbers of prices. They measure changes in the buying power of the dollar.

Nobody needs an index number to keep track of the length of the yardstick. That is a true standard. Money is not.

However friendly we feel toward dollars, however many pleasant things we say in their favor, however willing we are to take them in and let them work for us, we must admit that they have one failing. They are not 'the same yesterday, to-day, and forever.' At least, their purchasing power, which is all that concerns us, is not the same. And it is disappointing, to say the least, to lay away in a bank account a dollar which is in the pink of condition, only to find, when we go to take it out, that its ability to carry home a load of groceries has shrunk 50 per cent!

In recent years, however, thanks largely to the Federal Reserve System, the dollar in the United States has changed comparatively little in purchasing power. It has come nearer than ever before to being a true standard of value.

29

Gold as a Standard of Value

SOMETHING is needed for use as money which has great value in itself. Gold meets this test because it is in universal demand in the arts. In some countries, gold is still valued as highly for ornament as for money. A debutante in India joyously carries on her person thirty pounds of gold trimmings, with the reckless disregard for comfort that is shown by her fur-bearing sister on a warm day at Atlantic City.

The chief objection to gold as a basis of money is that it varies in value. In the United States, in 1896, a gold dollar would buy over 50 per cent more than in 1913. But in 1920 a gold dollar would buy less than half what it would buy in 1913. During one period, carpets came nearer than gold to being a 'standard' for measuring purchasing power, in the sense in which the yardstick is a 'standard' for measuring carpets. In other words, the exchange value of carpets in terms of boots, bon-bons, barrels, and commodities generally, varied much less than the exchange value of gold.

Money on a gold basis is a perfect standard of purchasing power for only one commodity; namely, gold. That is an advantage to dentists. They always know precisely how much gold a dollar will buy. But, unfortunately for a large proportion of the rest of us, it is almost always something else that we want to buy.

Nevertheless, the purchasing power of money in recent times has fluctuated less in gold-basis countries than in any others. Those countries which went off the gold basis during the War and after — Germany, for example, and Russia — suffered most. Their 'convertible' notes were merely fair-weather notes.

It is only in a hurricane, however, that a ship's anchor is fully tested; and it takes a World War to demonstrate whether a country's gold anchor is sufficient to keep the Ship of State from drifting away upon boundless seas of inconvertible paper.

The World Needs a Stable Dollar

BEFORE the World War a carpenter in Vienna loaned three thousand Austrian gold crowns, his total savings, the equivalent of a full year's wages. After the War the debtor returned to the carpenter, in full legal settlement, three thousand depreciated paper crowns — the wages of three days' labor. Thus does a shifting currency sweep away the savings of a life-time.

Still further to illustrate the instability of money, Joseph Szebenyei tells of a traveler in Vienna who offered the waiter, in a second-class restaurant, a twenty-dollar gold piece in payment for dinner. The bewildered waiter, after examining the treasure with curiosity and delight, went to the proprietor and said: 'Here is a gentleman, sir, who wants to pay with a twenty-dollar gold piece. How much am I to give for it?'

Having received instructions concerning rates of exchange, the waiter returned to the guest and said seriously: 'I am to give you as much change, sir, as you desire.' The full amount of paper money due as change was more, presumably, than the traveler could readily carry away with him.

These incidents show how far short money can come of being a standard of value. They show the difference between money income and real income.

Everybody now sees that inflation makes a mockery of thrift. When it takes five million marks to buy what one mark would buy a few years earlier, a millionaire has to spend his entire savings for one loaf of bread. Meanwhile, the savings of most widows, teachers, and clerks — in fact, of nearly everybody — cannot buy any bread at all. Even the comparatively slight changes in the value of the United States dollar, in the last fifteen years, have caused great injustice and suffering.

The world needs a stable dollar — one that will buy just about the same amount of goods, year in and year out.

Deflation is Worse Than Inflation

WHENEVER money increases much faster than the work which money has to perform, prices rise. The value of the dollar falls. That is inflation. Then there is an outcry against 'the high cost of living.' There is a demand for deflation.

But the remedy is worse than the disease; for deflation does not reduce the real cost of living; and it does bring evils of its own: bankruptcies, closed factories, ruined debtors, jobless fathers, hungry children.

Our muscles may be sore from climbing Pike's Peak, but we gain little relief from climbing down; only some more sore muscles. Business, which feels the glow of activity as it rushes forward, looks dejected when it has to go back. It brings to mind the horse that ran away, exhilarated by the exercise, but when forced to run all the way home, dropped dead at the stable door.

Eagerness for higher wages is natural; but higher wages are no benefit when prices rise faster than wages. Eagerness for lower prices is natural; but lower prices are no benefit when the currency is deflated and production is curtailed. For, no matter what happens to wages or to prices, people cannot long buy any more than they produce.

Theoretically, falling prices end all our troubles. Actually, they are the beginning of new troubles. For if there is any influence that is sure to force business men to cut down output, it is falling prices and the ever-present uncertainty as to how long they will keep on falling, and how far they will fall.

The greatest monetary need of the world is not 'abundant money,' not 'easy money,' not 'a more elastic supply of money,' but money that will stay put.

Both inflation and deflation are disastrous. Neither is a cure for the other.

Do We Want Low Prices?

WE must always keep in mind the distinction between *individual prices* and *the general price-level*. Otherwise, we shall get confused.

By *individual prices* we mean the value of any commodity or service — say a ton of coal or a ride in a taxicab — in terms of dollars. By *the general price-level* we mean a composite of all prices; that is to say, the cost of coal, taxicab rides, and everything else at one time or place, compared with the cost of the same commodities and services at another time or place.

Such comparisons we make by means of index numbers. Thus, if 100 stands for the wholesale commodity price-level of 1926, and if the level falls 3 per cent, the index number of wholesale commodity prices becomes 97. This tells us nothing about the change in the price of coal, or wheat, or good red herring, or any other single commodity. It may have fallen more or less than 3 per cent; or, by a rare chance, it may have fallen exactly 3 per cent.

Whether prices are high or low matters little. With prices twice as high, consumers can buy just as much as ever, provided wages and other income are twice as high. And business can proceed just as well on one price-level as on another, once prices have become stabilized on that level; just as a ship can sail as serenely and swiftly on Lake Superior as on the lower level of Lake Huron, once the ship has passed through the locks. It is the process of changing levels and the frequency of the change that retard progress.

When the price-level changes — that is to say, when the purchasing power of the dollar goes up or down — either the debtor or the creditor loses. But once the shift has been made, everybody gets along as well as ever. It makes hardly any difference where the price-level happens to be, as long as it stays where it is.

Is Money Wealth?

MEN used to think that the more money a country had, the more wealth that country would have. But it is easy to see that a country cannot increase its wealth merely by increasing its money. Suppose, by some magic, everybody found out, to-morrow morning, that he had twice as much money as he has to-night. That would make many men suddenly feel rich. But there would be no more things for money to buy; so each dollar would buy only about half as much as before.

To be sure, if you get a raise of five dollars a week in wages, and if the Government is not inflating the currency, those five dollars mean to you more potatoes, shoes, books, or something else. And for you, that is real wealth.

But it is different with a nation. No nation can increase its wealth by increasing its money. The *real* wealth of a nation is not in money, but in copper, machines, railroads, mines, forests.

The *real* income of a wage-earner also consists of goods. The scales show how many pounds of beef he brings home for dinner, but he does not eat the scales; and this relation between scales and a real meal is precisely the relation between dollar income and real income.

Money is a measure of a man's real income. This week it may comprise three quarts of milk, police protection, a daily newspaper, and so forth, to the end of a long list of commodities and services. But if you ask him the size of his income, he does not enumerate all these items. He sums them up by saying, 'Forty dollars a week.'

Nevertheless, real income, not money income, is the chief economic source of his satisfactions.

We should beware of any plan to turn out money more rapidly than we turn out real wealth. That is inflation. And that hurts everybody, especially wage-earners.

Why Not Print More Money?

HENRY FORD proposed to develop the power plant at Muscle Shoals, Alabama. The thirty millions of dollars necessary for this work, Mr. Ford declared, could be obtained from the printing-press, at little cost to the Government.

Mr. Ford was right, if only initial costs are considered; but he was wrong if he thought that he had discovered a new method of finance. The same plan was carried so far in the days of Wild-Cat Money that a Mississippi steamboat captain, who asked the price of firewood, received the answer, 'Cord for cord.' The same reliance on printer's ink brought Russia to the point where it took a bale of ruble notes to buy a hat.

Money will buy whatever is produced — not a particle more by any trick of alchemy, or legislation, or finance. After the Russians had multiplied their money two hundred and fifty-seven thousand times, they could not buy even as much with it as before, because they were producing less. When we print more money, there are no more goods for money to buy; not a single additional plow, or hat, or potato.

It follows that if the Government prints money to lend to farmers or to anybody else, free of charge, thereby increasing the money in circulation without increasing the goods that money will buy, some people gain at the expense of the rest of us.

If the printing-press is all a country needs for thirty *millions* of dollars, why not thirty *billions?* If one plant is a sufficient basis for currency, why not a thousand plants? With such boundless issues of paper dollars, our own policy would differ in no way from the Lenin policy of paying bills with the printing-press — a method first employed, according to Goethe's *Faust*, by the Devil.

A French proverb says: 'After the printing-press, the guillotine.'

'A Nightmare of Panics'

IT is said that the total wealth of the United States is more than 240 billions. But the total currency in circulation is only eight billions.

'It is therefore evident,' we are told, 'that only one thirtieth of the wealth of the country could be liquidated in money at any given time. Is it any wonder that we suffer periodically from a nightmare of panics?'

The argument seems to be that if we had thirty times as much money in circulation, the total national wealth — all the rabbits, railroads, radishes, and everything else — could be sold at the same moment.

And so all our financial troubles would be over!

That is sheer nonsense. In the first place, nobody wants to sell the total wealth at any given time. There are always some persons who are willing to keep their houses, furniture, books, even their saxophones and brown derbies, at least for a few days longer. There are also some corporations which are not for sale.

Perhaps only one thirtieth of the population, at any given time, could ride on railroads or talk on telephones. But there is no 'nightmare of panics' on that account.

Even if we did suddenly increase the money in circulation thirty-fold, we should not be any better prepared to exchange our wealth; for the wealth itself would have increased at least thirty-fold in dollar-values. Prices would have gone up as they did in Russia.

As prices went up, more and more money would be needed, not to increase the volume of trade, but merely to carry on the existing volume. If we suddenly increased thirty-fold the money in circulation, we should not thereby insure ourselves against a 'nightmare of panics.' On the contrary, we should invite one.

Edison-Ford Commodity Money

MR. EDISON and Mr. Ford advocate 'Commodity Money.' Their idea is to have the Government store wheat, tobacco, and other products, and issue money to farmers 'representing' these products. Long ago we rejected free coinage of silver. Now the demand comes for the free coinage of turnips and tripe and everything else.

If coins or paper dollars are limited merely by what they 'represent,' they may as well represent the estimated number of fish in the ocean. Unless 'representation' means *convertibility*, on demand, into something freely accepted for goods the world over, the commodity basis does not guarantee the value of money. History has proved this over and over again.

All the world freely accepts gold. All the world knows precisely what is meant by the convertibility of a paper dollar into 25.8 grains of gold. But what is meant by the convertibility of a 'Commodity Dollar' into, let us say, one millionth part of the corn, apples, and so forth, stored in Government warehouses? How could the holder of the dollar collect his share? What could he do with it?

If a warehouse full of tobacco guarantees the soundness of the notes that are issued against it, these notes must be redeemable in tobacco. They are, in fact, Federal Tobacco notes. The plan must provide, in like manner, for Federal Flax notes, Federal Salt Fish notes, and so forth. Furthermore, there would have to be as many kinds of Salt Fish notes as there were kinds of salt fish. Every one would need to have at hand the latest commodity quotations in order to estimate the value of different kinds of dollars. Everybody would have to observe whether he had Kippered Herring notes or Salt Cod notes.

Evidently, commodity notes could not serve the purpose of money.

Money Based on Land

A PLAN has been proposed in Congress to solve 'The Farm Problem' by issuing money 'representing' farm lands. Why not? If a farmer needs money to buy seed, why should not the Government issue new currency, based on land?

The French people tried this plan at the time of the Revolution. They called the money *assignats*. At first 7,000 millions were issued; a few months later 16,000 millions, and presently 45,000 millions. To maintain the value of this land currency, the law declared that any one who gave or accepted it at less than face value, should spend twenty years in irons. In spite of the law, the holder of a 'land' note, said to be worth five dollars, was lucky if he could pass it off for two cents.

Massachusetts had the same experience when it issued land-currency in colonial days. Likewise Japan.

The trouble is easy to see. As soon as we issue money against land, we increase our money, but not our land. Therefore, money falls in purchasing power, and land rises in dollar-value. Consequently, land has a higher loan-value; and so serves as the basis for even larger issues of money. But as these new issues still further increase the dollar-values of land, land serves as the basis for still further issues of money. And so on, without limit. You cannot hold a ship in place by making it fast to a drifting ship.

The whole world knows exactly what is meant by the convertibility of a paper dollar into a fixed weight of gold. But what is meant by the convertibility of a paper dollar into land? What is meant by a unit of land? Where could the holder of money get it, and what could he do with it? Who would accept it in exchange? How could it be sent across the ocean to settle international balances? Nobody questions the value of land for certain purposes, but for monetary purposes it is more cumbersome than cows.

'Labor-Hours' as Money

THOSE who favor the 'labor-hour' as a unit of money say that, since all wealth is the product of labor, labor should be the basis of money. They contend that every man should be able to exchange the product of an hour of his labor, for the product of an hour of labor of any other man. Thus, if it takes a hatter three hours to make a hat, he should receive three exchange-units; and they should entitle him to anything, say a book, that was made in three hours.

But how can we tell how many hours it took to produce a book? How long did it take to make the ink? How many minutes of the labor of the author are to be charged to each copy of the book? How much of the time of the fireman who stoked the engine that hauled the car that carried the pulp that went to the mill that made the paper the book used? We should have to go even farther before we could find all the miners, typists, bank clerks, freight agents, postmen, fishermen, salesmen, and so on, whose labor helped to produce that book.

There are other difficulties. What is to be done with all the products that nobody will buy at the fixed price — the books that nobody wants, the cakes that were burned, the hats that are out of style? How, on the other hand, are goods to be allotted when demand exceeds supply? Which lovers of art are to be allowed to exchange their labor, hour for hour, for the labor of our greatest portrait painter? Somebody must decide.

Again, when all wages are the same, why should any one choose the hard or the disagreeable jobs? Another objection is the chief objection to Communism. The longer a man took to make a hat, the more labor-hour checks he would receive for making it. Efficiency would soon become an historic virtue. Finally, the labor-hour unit would be more unstable in value than cows, or nails, or hides.

The plan does not work, as Russia quickly found out.

The Philosopher's Stone

SOME men believe that a long-trend fall in commodity prices is inevitable because of a world shortage in the production of gold. They point out the fact — and it is a fact — that the annual increase in the world's supply of monetary gold is less than the annual increase in the world's volume of trade.

The supply of gold, however, had little to do with the fall of commodity prices in the United States during 1929 and 1930. While prices were falling, gold reserves were rising.

During the year 1929, moreover, Great Britain and Germany lost about 140 millions of monetary gold; whereas France and the United States gained about 530 millions. Yet wholesale prices fell 7 or 8 per cent in France and in the United States, but fell only 4 per cent in Great Britain and in Germany.

No, the gold supply was not the cause of falling prices in the United States.

Sometime in the distant future, it is true, we may not have enough gold to maintain the price-level, under our present monetary system. But that system was devised by man to suit his needs. It has been improved, time and again, to meet his changing needs. Ways have been found of making a given stock of gold do more work. Other ways will be found in the future.

It would be stupid to resign ourselves to the depressing influence of a prolonged fall in prices, if it turns out that we have devised a system under which prices *must* fall.

Perhaps we cannot, by taking thought, transmute lead into gold; for in spite of centuries of search, we do not have the benefit of the Philosopher's Stone.

But we can, by taking thought, make a given volume of gold support a larger volume of money, and thus sustain the price-level. For we *do* have the benefit of the Philosopher's Brain.

When the Engine Stalls

IT is said that the use of a gold basis for money is merely a concession to human weakness. It is. So, for that matter, is the use of jails. If human beings were different, and if politicians could be counted on to act with wisdom, it might be possible to get along without the gold basis of money.

No arrangement is ideal which requires us to hoard vast stores of gold and to carry them back and forth across the ocean. But there is no immediate need of devising an ideal system, for there are no ideal men to use it. If all men were honest, we could do away with vaults and prison bars, and thus save tons of iron and steel. War is utter waste. If nations were sufficiently wise, they would get on without huge armaments. Some day they will. The gold basis also involves waste. If nations were sufficiently wise, they would do without that.

But nations are *not* sufficiently wise to abolish at once their prisons, or armaments, or gold reserves. Men and women being what they are, no nation has kept its paper money within bounds, except by means of an arbitrary restraint. And the gold standard has proved to be the best restraint.

It is stupid to insist that everything is all right when, every now and then, there seems to be no way of letting idle machines, materials, men, and money go on with the work of feeding, housing, and clothing us. Something really is wrong.

But when an engine stalls, a mechanic cannot set it in motion by seizing a hammer and pounding the engine in the wrong place. Valuable time is wasted, attention is diverted from the right place, and the machinery is injured. Meanwhile, the bungling mechanic works himself into such bad temper that there is less prospect than ever of finding the real trouble. To attack the gold basis of money is to hammer our economic machinery in the wrong place.

Is Money Worthy of Its Hire?

'M R. FORD thinks it is stupid, and so do I,' says Mr. Edison, speaking of the Muscle Shoals project, 'that for the loan of $30,000,000 of their own money the people of the United States should be compelled to pay $66,000,000. That is what it amounts to, with interest. People who will not turn a shovelful of dirt nor contribute a pound of material will collect more money from the United States than will the people who supply the material and do the work. That is the terrible thing about interest.'

Is there really anything more terrible about paying for the use of money than about paying for the use of anything else? Suppose Sam Witham needs a harvesting machine, and has no money. He can either borrow a machine of Neighbor Brown, or borrow money and buy a machine. The machine is his neighbor's capital goods. The money is a claim upon capital goods.

Sam would not expect to borrow a machine, without in some way paying for the use of the machine. Why should he expect to borrow money — which will buy the same machine — without paying for the use of the money?

Now, suppose that Sam uses the machine so successfully that he has a thousand dollars' profit. With that money he can buy more land, and he can let Neighbor Brown have the use of the land. Neighbor Brown, naturally, would expect to pay rent.

Instead of buying the land, however, Sam could lend the thousand dollars to his neighbor, in order that his neighbor might buy the land. In that case Neighbor Brown should expect to pay rent for the money.

Plainly, it is just as fair to charge for the use of money as to charge for the use of things that money will buy. Money is worthy of its hire.

Why Not Abolish Government Bonds?

WHY should the Government pay interest?

'If the Government issued money on its own account,' says a popular weekly, 'it would eliminate that choice bit of investment paper — the Government bond. No Government bonds — no public debt — and there would be no interest.'

What would that lead to? Let us see.

When public expenses exceed public revenues, there are two ways of paying the bills: by borrowing money and by printing money. When a government borrows money, it must pay whatever interest is necessary to obtain the money. And so far as it borrows savings, it does not inflate the currency. But when a government pays its deficits by printing money, it inflates the currency. That reduces the value of every dollar a man has saved. So, by paying deficits with the printing-press, the Government confiscates savings instead of borrowing them. That policy brought Russia to financial chaos.

For your Government to spend money which is not the savings of its people is as bad as it is for you to sign checks without having first deposited money in the bank.

Nor does inflating the currency reduce interest rates. In all her history, Germany never had as much money, or as high interest rates, as she had immediately following the World War. In the United States, also, interest rates went up, even though the volume of money increased. Then, after the bubble of monetary inflation burst in 1920, and again after the stock market crash in 1929, the supply of money was reduced, yet interest rates went down. Money, unlike wheat and motor cars, is not easier to obtain simply because the total supply is increased.

No country can lower the rent of money merely by printing a lot of it.

Capitalism 'Delivers the Goods'

IF you own a Ford car, you have no doubt that Henry Ford, while making large profits, benefited all of us. He provided us with millions of automobiles and with gigantic factories. Both the cars and the factories are to some extent community gain.

What Mr. Ford has done on a large scale, thousands of enterprisers have done on a small scale. All these men have increased our productive resources. No matter who owns this new capital, it helps everybody.

On the other hand, any one man may realize profits without benefiting the rest of us. In so far as he profits by holding unimproved lands, by manipulating the stock market, by bribing public officers, by floating securities of useless corporations, or by destroying needed enterprises, he makes gains, but the community does not.

How, then, shall we deal with profit-makers? Evidently, we cannot deal justly with them until we distinguish between those who add to community wealth and those who do not.

In any event, we must admit that it is profit-seekers who have made possible our present high standard of living. The epoch in which the profit motive became dominant was the one that brought the most effective use of new inventions and the most rapid increase in real wages. No other period in the world's history showed such progress in public health, in medicine, in free schools, in transportation, and, generally speaking, in the means of gratifying human wants. Furthermore, the greatest progress has been made in those countries where the profit motive has been most highly developed.

'It may be freely admitted,' according to Sidney and Beatrice Webb, British Socialists, 'that, with all its drawbacks, the dictatorship of the capitalist scored an initial success. It delivered the goods.'

The Mainspring of Business

THERE are many ways of making a living, but nearly all of them depend on profits. Most of us, it is true, live on wages; but wages depend largely on profits. Employers, as a rule, pay wages only with the expectation of making profits; and, unless these expectations are realized, wages *must* stop.

If the mainspring of your watch is broken, you can wind it until the cows come home without making the watch go. The mainspring of business is *Profits*. The hope of profits drives the life-sustaining blood to every part of the economic body. The blood is money.

When the hope of profits wanes, the flow of money wanes. The central pumping station gets out of order. It cannot develop sufficient power to keep money circulating and men employed. Whether we like it or not, that is a fact.

We can imagine an industrial society in which the profit motive has been replaced by some other motive. We can imagine a human body in which a new kind of pump has taken the place of the heart. But it would require more than a major operation to create either of these new organisms.

Even those people who want to abolish the profit motive, admit its power. Even Karl Marx, in his *Communist Manifesto* of 1848, long before the present era of great industries, admitted that the pursuit of profits had 'created more massive and more colossal productive forces than had all preceding generations together.'

What would Karl Marx think if he could visit the United States to-day! No doubt he would be amazed at the reduction in the hours of labor and increase in the rewards of labor. And he would have to admit that this achievement — for the sake of which he wanted to abolish profits — has resulted largely from the pursuit of profits.

Why Not Abolish Profits?

MOST of us make a living out of profits. Not merely the people who run stores and factories, but everybody who draws wages. Fully forty million of us in this country depend for a livelihood upon the ability of the concerns for which we work to operate at a profit.

A report of the General Electric Company shows that out of each dollar of income, the Company pays, directly, about 41 cents as wages, and about 5 cents as cash dividends. Of course it is the 41 cents of wages that make the 5 cents of dividends possible. On the other hand, it is the 5 cents that make the 41 cents possible. The profit keeps the business going, and thus enables the workers to collect their pay.

When Thoreau fled from the profit-making world which he detested to his hut on the shore of Walden Pond, he carried an axe on his shoulder. An axe made and sold at a profit — symbol of the established economic order which he was trying to escape!

Even John Burroughs, with his delight in meadow-larks and goldenrod, owed much of his joy, to say nothing of his comfort, to mills and mines, printshops and plantations, that ministered to his welfare only as long as they realized profits.

For many years a company manufactured a popular soap powder. Management was efficient. Profits were substantial. Then demand slackened. Profits dwindled — vanished. The firm shut up shop, and workers were deprived of the chance to make a living.

To make steadier progress, we must run the whole machinery of business more smoothly, avoid breakdowns, reduce wastes, adjust output to demand — in short, help to stabilize profits.

That will help to stabilize jobs and payrolls.

'Something for Nothing'

ANY one who pockets business profits,' says a New York professor, 'obtains something for nothing.'

Is that strictly true? Suppose a man lends anything — buildings, money wherewith to buy them, money to advance as wages; in short, capital in any form. In every case he contributes something and runs the risk of losing it. If, instead of losing what he lends, he gains a profit, it cannot be said that he has obtained something for nothing.

A farmer who lends his tractor to a neighbor, and receives part of the income as a reward, knows that he is not receiving something for nothing. An engineer who deposits his savings in a Brotherhood bank, does not regard the interest he receives as something for nothing.

Now, there is no essential difference between lending a man capital goods and lending him the money wherewith to buy capital goods; or between lending to one man and lending to an organization of men. Nor does it matter whether the organization is called a bank, or a coöperative society, or a corporation. In every case there is risk of loss.

Risks are universal. For the orange grower, there is danger of a frost; for the cotton planter, the boll weevil; for the bond buyer, inflation; for the milliner, changes in style; for the contractor, strikes; for the railroads, Congress. The prospector drills where there may be no oil. The street railway company constructs a line that the automobile may put out of business. The maker of phonographs goes cheerfully ahead. Then comes the radio!

So it is the world over. Every business faces not only risks that are the common lot, but also risks that are peculiarly its own. To induce any one to take these risks there must be a prospect of gain. If the gain is realized, it is not 'something for nothing'; it is a reward for risk-bearing.

Business Risks *vs.* Gambling Risks

EVERYBODY can see that some money gains are due mainly to chance. By chance we mean occurrences wholly beyond the control or prediction of those who benefit by them.

Such are the profits of a man who buys a ranch, with no thought of using it for anything but a ranch, and then finds that it is rich in oil. Most of the profits which result from rising prices are profits of chance. Indeed, every one of us, especially in an era of 'bull markets,' has observed men who profit from 'bull luck.' Every one knows of men who sow where they do not reap, and of men who reap where they do not sow.

As a matter of fact, *all* profits result partly from chance. It is not possible to find a business success which can be ascribed wholly to labor, ability, wisdom, and devotion. The outcome of every commercial enterprise depends on changes in weather, population, tastes, legislation, and other factors which men can neither control nor forecast.

All business men, in order to make profits, must take business risks. They need not, however, take gambling risks. In the construction of the Yankee Stadium, numerous risks were involved; the risk of injury to workmen, for example. This risk was part and parcel of the enterprise; somebody had to carry it. But nobody *has* to bet on the outcome of a ball game.

In placing a bet, the gambler *creates* a risk. In placing an employers' liability policy, the insurance company *takes over* an existing risk.

Gambling is taking chances on artificial risks. Such risks, at Monte Carlo or elsewhere, are not a necessary part of business. Economically, society does not care whether the race-track gambler bets on Fire-Fly or on Spark-Plug, or on neither.

Somebody must assume business risks. Nobody need assume gambling risks.

The Price of Progress

BUSINESS losses are, in part, the price we have to pay for progress. The money that is invested in getting ready to produce a new colored movie, a new magazine, a new frozen-foods device, or a new oil heater, may be a total loss, because somebody reaches the market first with a better product. Corner grocers fail because chain stores develop cheaper distribution. Wooden ships rot at the wharves because faster ships take their places. Textbooks are discarded because better books are written. Even new machines sometimes become obsolete and are scrapped before they have ever been used.

Such losses could be avoided only in a static — a changeless — society. But the industrial society in which we live is dynamic. Rapidly it is becoming more and more dynamic.

It is a society in which consumers are free to choose and producers are free to compete for their dollars. In such a world, business must run risks and suffer losses. Somebody has to pay these losses. In the present industrial order, they are paid by a comparatively few people, as a penalty for their failures in business.

In any other industrial order, losses would occur. Radical reformers may overlook this problem in theory, but they could not overlook it in practice. Even under communism, there would be risks and mistakes, and therefore losses. These losses would be distributed over the whole population.

To be sure, a government could avoid losses in any one industry by operating it as a monopoly, fixing prices, and paying deficits out of tax receipts. In this way, the United States Government covered the losses incurred by its management of the railroads. But no government could operate *all* industries that way.

Every progressive society in some way has to meet business losses. That is part of the price of progress.

The Farm Problem

THE 'farm problem' persists partly because farmers persist in raising more produce than can be sold at satisfactory prices. There is only one cure for this kind of over-production. That cure is reduction of crop acreage.

How is this reduction to be brought about? The only economically sound way is through the operation of economic law. In the interests of common welfare, those farmers should reduce acreage who are farming at the greatest disadvantage. The high-cost producer should give way to the low-cost producer. Leave them alone and that is what will happen.

It is happening every day in numerous industries. The most efficient makers of automobiles, for example, are putting the least efficient out of business. There is the same struggle for existence among producers of copper, kegs, cotton cloth, tin cans, wood pulp, and thousands of other commodities.

The law of supply and demand, functioning through price, eliminates those growers of farm products who are least fit to survive. They are what economists call 'marginal producers.' To protect them from the operation of the law of supply and demand is to obstruct the forces which make for higher per capita production and higher standards of living.

The Federal Farm Board tried another way to reduce crop acreage. The Board recommended that all wheat growers, regardless of efficiency, reduce their acreage ten per cent. The Board also advised a general reduction of cotton acreage.

The farmers, of course, did not accept this advice. And they should not. Those who are growing wheat at lowest cost should *not* cut down acreage. The reduction should come through the elimination of the marginal producer. This takes place without the advice of the Government.

And it benefits everybody, including farmers.

Capital Often Works for Nothing

PROPERTY rights,' we are told, 'give property owners a prior claim on production. The risks of industry and the losses are borne in the first instance by labor.'

As far as profits and dividends are concerned, this is far from the truth. Wages not only have a prior claim, but are actually paid, as a rule, before it is possible to tell whether there will be any profits.

Starting with the assumption that winds always blow steadily in one direction, we can develop an extraordinary theory of aeronautics. But it will not help us to fly. Upon the assumption that business can always be conducted at a profit, we can construct in imagination an extraordinary industrial society. But it will not work.

At the end even of a prosperous year, more than 100,000 corporations, having paid wages throughout the year, find that there is nothing left for dividends. From 1913 to 1927 the New York, New Haven, and Hartford Railroad carried millions of people, and the necessities of life to millions more. During these fourteen years, the road paid wages regularly. Yet throughout this long period, the owners of the road received not a single dollar in dividends.

As a matter of fact, the losses which result from business depressions fall more heavily on stockholders than on wage-earners. Capital often works without income. Labor rarely works without wages.

The job and the income of the laborer should be more secure. Industry must conquer involuntary unemployment. There is no question about that. But it will not help matters to over-look the insecurity of capital income. Capital, too, suffers from involuntary unemployment. Both capital and labor should and can attain greater security of incomes.

Conspiracies to Limit Production

THE cost of living is high,' we are told, 'because producers are in conspiracy to limit production in order to maintain prices.'

How can this be? It is only under complete monopoly, or agreements that really bind all the producers of a given commodity, that total output can possibly be subject to control. There is no such control of the production of leather, bread, fur coats, nails, chairs, ice cream, watches, and thousands of other familiar articles. An agreement to limit the output of such things would be difficult to arrange, and the temptation to violate the agreement would be strong. In any event, the legal prosecution of violators would be impossible, because the agreement to maintain prices would be illegal.

The reason why each producer would be tempted to break his word is plain enough. It is because the profits of the individual producer usually increase with the volume of *his* business. He would like to have his competitors produce less, but there is no point in limiting *his* output.

No one imagines that the makers of Buick cars, for example, ever produce fewer cars, for the purpose of maintaining prices, when Chrysler factories are running at capacity. That case is typical. In the face of such competition, every producer who knows his business is striving to produce more goods, at lower costs, and to sell them at lower prices. He knows that the chief result of limiting his output would be to give a larger share of the market to his competitors.

That is why limitation of output is rarely the result of conspiracy to maintain prices. Usually, it is the outcome of the independent decisions of thousands of producers, each of whom must produce no more than he can sell at a profit, or run the risk of bankruptcy.

Why Blame the Profit-Seekers?

UNDER the sabotage of the profit system,' complains a
college professor, 'basic production languishes, while the
production of non-essentials flourishes. Ford can make more
cars and the tobacco men more cigarettes, but the farmers must
stop growing wheat and apples.'

We were not aware that the farmers had stopped growing
apples; and we were under the impression that the Government
was encouraging the farmers to grow more wheat, by using
public funds to keep up the price. But those are mere details.
The professor, we assume, is not especially interested in wheat
and apples. His idea seems to be that if we were only free from
the shackles of the profit system, we could go ahead indefinitely
increasing the output of everything.

Such a course, however, would be stupid. If the farmers
grow less wheat, it is not because Mr. Ford is wickedly seeking
more profits, but because the people would rather buy more
cars than eat more bread. Under *any* system, it would be
necessary to make less of what people do *not* particularly want,
in order to make more of what they *do* want.

That is precisely what producers under the profit system are
now doing every day. Every day millions of us, in buying one
thing instead of another, express our relative desires, not only
for automobiles, tobacco, wheat, and apples, but for everything
else that is offered for sale. Profit-seekers act accordingly.
They make more of what we especially want; less of other
things. If they make more cars and cigarettes, and raise fewer
apples and less wheat, they do so under orders from consumers.
And, as a rule, they must either obey these orders or go out of
business.

But why blame the profit-seekers?

What Determines Rate of Profit?

THERE is no such thing as a normal rate of profit even among producers of the same commodity. To see why this must be true, we have only to take into account three facts.

First, profit is the difference between selling price and cost.

Second, the selling price of a given commodity must be virtually the same, as a rule, no matter who produces it, provided buyers are free to compete for the product in an open market.

Third, for no two producers of the same thing — cartridges or copper, cotton cloth or cabbages — is the cost of production, by any chance, exactly the same.

It follows that the profits of a given producer are determined mainly by the relation of his costs to the costs of his competitors.

To illustrate. A few years ago three companies produced virtually the same machine, A at a lower cost than B, and B at a lower cost than C. The buyers of the machine, of course, were not interested in the high costs of C. They paid the same price to all three producers. As a result, A made a profit of 12 per cent, B made a profit of 2 per cent, and C suffered a loss of 3 per cent. The high profits of Company A resulted chiefly from high efficiency. To be sure, Company A might have wasted labor or materials, or otherwise reduced its efficiency, in order to bring its profits down; but this would not appeal to anybody as a service to society. It would not help consumers, for it would neither increase the supply nor decrease the price.

Unless there is interference by the Government or other arbitrary control, the price is fixed by what consumers pay for the product of the highest-cost producer who turns out any part of the necessary supply. It is the inefficiency or unfavorable position of the high-cost producer which enables the low-cost producer to make a high rate of profit.

The 'Normal Rate of Profit'

MANY proposals for taxing business, regulating prices, and fixing tariff rates are based on the belief that there is a normal rate of profit. As a matter of fact, profits vary widely. War and the weather, fashions and finance, politics and business cycles do not have the same effect on the profits of any two industries, or any two companies.

For example, not long ago annual profits in the canning industry rose from 4 per cent to 32 per cent, and then fell to 15 per cent. Profits of shoe manufacturers are twice as high in some years as in others. The quarterly profits of motor companies fell at one time from seven million to nothing at all, and then rose to several times seven million. Leather concerns lost 10 per cent in 1921, gained 3 per cent in 1922, fell back the next year to a loss of 4 per cent, and have not yet found out what 'normal' means. An industry exempt from sudden shifts of fortune is almost as rare as a windmill free from sudden shifts of air.

Profits also vary widely among different concerns in the same field. In a single year, the fortunes of automobile makers have ranged from a loss of 75 per cent to a gain of 15 per cent. In a single year, the earnings of commercial banks have ranged from nothing at all to 75 per cent. In fact, it is impossible to find a company in any freely competitive field with a 'typical' profit and loss record. Profits of industry as a whole also go up and down like a roller-coaster. Unlike population and production, profits as a whole do not show a steady rate of growth. Unlike interest rates, profit rates do not cluster closely around an average.

What, then, is the normal rate of profit? There is no such thing. We might as well ask: What is the normal temperature on Fridays?

Who Pays for Advertising?

HAVE you a Little Depressant in your home? Have you a bright-eyed observer who says she doesn't know anything about 'economics' except that, whatever else it is, it isn't 'economical'?

If you have such a guide through the mazes of costs and profits, she will open the latest weekly from Philadelphia some day and exclaim, 'What an attractive ad! Six colors, and endorsed by a Rear-Admiral! Here is his picture. But who pays for it?'

Then she will add triumphantly, 'You do!'

Well, as a matter of fact, you *do*, as you knew all the time. That is to say, consumers pay for advertising, as they pay for everything else. They have to pay, because 'consumers' includes all of us, and there is nobody except all of us to pay for anything.

But consumers pay for that particular advertisement — that beautiful six-color picture of the Rear-Admiral — only if they like it well enough to buy what it advertises. If, on the other hand, it doesn't stir them to act, they don't pay for it at all.

Who, then, does pay for it? The unfortunate manufacturer who ran the risk. You are free to buy his product, and thus help him pay for calling it to your attention. Or you may yawn, turn over a page, and let him call his product to your attention wholly at his own expense.

If the Little Depressant gets a melancholy satisfaction out of the belief that she is helping to subsidize commercial artists, don't disillusion her. But if she is worried, explain to her that no advertiser can possibly tell in advance whether or not consumers will pay for his particular advertising. Sometimes they do pay; but sometimes it is the owners of the business who pay, as they do for all errors of management.

Gulf Between Labor and Capital

THE Bolshevists who were caught in China conspiring to overthrow the Chinese Government explained that they were merely trying to destroy capitalism. In this country, also, there are aliens who are merely trying to do that. They are cussing capitalism in seventy-six known languages, and in several others which have not yet been identified.

Why did they come to this country? Chiefly because of our high standard of living.

And how was that achieved? Through capitalism. Achieved, in other words, because some far-sighted persons saved money and invested it — invested it in the hope of receiving rent, interest, and dividends. Unless some human beings, sometime in the past, had saved, and had founded a safe social order in which to invest their savings, we should all be fighting wild beasts with our bare hands, traveling in mud, and lighting our dismal dugouts with candles — or not at all. That seems to be reason enough for trying to induce *everybody* to save and invest — that is, to become capitalists.

We cannot get along without labor; we cannot get along without capital. We should all become laborers; we should all become capitalists.

The War brought us nearer to that goal, for it shoved many idlers into action, and it created several million more capitalists — owners of Government bonds. In the past few years several million other workers have become capitalists through the purchase of stocks.

These new owners of industry understand that, every time they clip a coupon or receive a dividend, they are reaping the just rewards of their thrift, and that all rewards for thrift depend on protection of private property and respect for law.

Some day everybody may understand that. Some day the gulf between labor and capital may become an imaginary line.

Who Fixed the Price of Your Hat?

WHO fixed the price of your hat? You did. The seller merely fixed the price at which the hat was *offered*. You fixed the price at which it was *sold*.

Selling prices are not made by the simple process of adding profits to costs. In the long run, it is true, prices tend to keep above costs. Otherwise, business would stop, as surely as a motor car stops when the fuel gives out. But at any given time, in the case of any given commodity already produced, buyers fix the price.

This is shown in the Automatic Bargain Basement of a Boston store, where customers are invited to make their own prices. If they refuse to pay the price at which goods are offered, that price, after twelve days, is reduced 25 per cent. If buyers hold out six days more, the price is reduced 50 per cent; in another six days, 75 per cent; and six days later, the goods are given away.

So the customers all wait for the markdowns!

If you think so, you forget that in the automatic basement, as in every other part of the store, buyers are competing with each other for the same goods. If a buyer waits for a markdown on the particular coat that has taken his fancy, some other buyer may get the coat. As a rule, the buyer does not wait. About 85 per cent of the automatic basement stocks are sold at the first offering price.

But, it is said, buyers *have* to buy something or starve. Even so, the rule holds. Whether it is caviar or corn, the price is fixed by those who buy that, instead of something else.

No merchant ever suffers long under the delusion that he controls prices. In filling out price tags he merely guesses what buyers will pay. If he guesses wrong, he has to guess again. His cash register tells him when he guesses right.

The merchant who sold you your hat guessed right.

Prices Decide Who Gets the Goods

YES, it is the buyer who fixes the price. Of course the price is unsatisfactory. No price can be low enough to satisfy all buyers individually, as long as collectively they want more goods than there are.

This brings us to the most fundamental of all economic facts: Human beings have their own notions about what they want; and there is never enough of what they want to go around. This is the origin of all economic problems.

If there were a given number of units of goods and precisely the same number of buyers, and if each buyer would be satisfied with one unit, economics would present no difficulties. Price would lose its sting, and competition its victories. Indeed, price would have no meaning.

But the moment there are only one hundred units of goods, and one hundred and one human beings who want them, competition begins. As long as this competition continues, there must be some means of determining *who* gets the goods.

Few things that human beings want are as free as air. Scarcity is the rule. Antagonism of interests is the result. This antagonism is too deep to be overcome by any political program whatever. Socialists and communists do not overcome it; they merely overlook it. They can indulge in this oversight, however, only as long as they confine themselves to theory. As soon as they try their ideas in practice, this conflict of interests thrusts itself rudely into the middle of things, and gums up the whole works.

The established price and profit economy, on the other hand, does not blink the facts. It accepts human beings as they are. Under this system, consumers compete daily in price markets for limited supplies of goods.

And prices decide who gets the goods.

When Are Prices Right?

BUYERS compete with one another for the same goods. Price is the product of that competition.

Profit and loss are by-products.

One of the functions of price is to move goods. Sometimes it moves them at a loss to the seller; sometimes, at a profit.

When prices do *not* move goods into consumers' hands at the right rate, there is general *over*production of goods. And that, of course, is merely another name for general *under*consumption.

When prices do *not* move goods, business suffers a depression; and it does not get over it until prices again fulfill their function. Then prices are right — economically right.

There is a right humidity for making cloth, a right temperature for baking bread, a right current for a given motor. In each case the rightness can be proved by measurement, but not by personal opinion. Similarly, the extent to which prices function is a question of fact. They either do or they do not move goods.

We say, 'When prices are right, we shall buy.' We should be closer to the truth if we said: 'When we buy, prices are right.' Prices are right when buyers buy. There is no other test.

An adding machine can do nothing to comfort the bankrupt. Its function is not to sympathize with him, but to sum up his losses. The function of price is not to supplement the Red Cross, but to move goods. Prices are economic, not charitable institutions. It is no use finding fault with them because they fail to do what they are not intended to do. For the purposes of pleasure-riding, there is something wrong with a steam-roller; but morally there is nothing wrong. Prices always are wrong for bringing relief to the destitute, but they are not morally wrong.

The only crime prices can commit is to fail to move goods.

Why Not Fix the Price of Leather?

THIS year's convention of the Tanners' Council sounded much like last year's. Here is the sad story, as it is told at every Tanners' Convention:

The tanners are engaged in a fundamental industry. Leather is a necessity. Yet in this essential industry, not one year out of three is profitable. The prices of what the tanners have to sell go down, while the prices of what they have to buy go up. Every year many tanners sell leather at a loss in a weak market, when they should have held it over for sale at a profit in a strong market. The capacity of the country for producing leather increases faster than the consumer demand for leather. The tanners could sell their leather at a profit every year if they would refrain from over-producing; but they always over-produce.

To one of the visitors at the Tanners' Convention this year, the whole sad story sounded familiar. He had heard substantially the same story, over and over again, at meetings of farmers. So he proposed that the tanners petition Congress to form a Federal Leather Board, empowered to use a hundred million dollars of tax-payers' money to buy up surplus leather and stabilize the price.

Did the tanners arise as one man and cheer the proposal? They did not. They had too much sense. They knew that their troubles had come largely from supplying leather beyond the demand. They knew that the one certain result of boosting the price of surplus leather with Federal funds would be the production of still more surplus leather. They knew that every attempt of the Government to fix prices is economically unsound.

The farmers have not yet found that out. But they will.

Are Stock Prices Too High?

THE chief purpose of the Federal Reserve System is to maintain an ample supply of sound money, so that producers may go forward confidently on a stable commodity price-level. On the whole, the System has served that purpose well — exceedingly well. There has been no shortage of capital.

To achieve that end, however, is to increase *real* wages, *real* profits, *real* capital — in short, *real* prosperity — and therefore the *real* values of common stocks. *Real* values are much higher than they were a few years ago. Nobody doubts that. How much higher? Again, how large a volume of brokers' loans is necessary to take care of *sound* business on this new level? What, after all, *is* the proper basis for capitalizing the prospective earnings of corporations?

These questions we must answer before we can tell, at any time, whether the general level of stock prices is too high. They are all quantitative questions. They can be answered by measurements, but not by opinions.

We do not argue concerning the pressure of steam; we consult a gauge. We do not take a vote concerning the number of cases of smallpox; we count them.

Yet some of the questions of finance we seem to think we can settle by guesses and opinions. Many people 'guess' stock prices are too high and brokers' loans 'excessive,' merely because they are much higher than they used to be. By the same token, wages are excessive; savings are excessive; capital is excessive; scientific knowledge is excessive. In short, wealth is excessive. And stock certificates merely represent this wealth.

How much are they worth? Nobody knows. If any one acts on a belief that stock prices are too high, or too low, he acts upon an opinion.

Seats for the Harvard-Yale Game

EVERY fall, about fifty-seven thousand seats for the Harvard-Yale football game are sold, but not to the highest
bidders. The seats are allotted to a favored list at a fixed price.
Those who receive them are not allowed to resell them, on
penalty of being black-listed and denied tickets in the future.

The object of the black-list is to prevent speculation. If
Harvard-Yale tickets were sold as most things are sold, all but
fifty-seven thousand bidders would be eliminated. What the
price would be, nobody knows; perhaps fifty dollars; perhaps a
hundred and fifty dollars. The bidding would provide another
means of scrambling after social prestige, another exhibition
ground for those who love conspicuous waste.

Since bidding is not allowed, the seats have to be distributed
on some other basis.

But pig-iron, cigars, diamonds, and a hundred thousand other
things for which buyers compete with each other, cannot be
distributed at fixed prices by the Harvard-Yale ticket plan.
The Government could not fix prices for all these things, declare
them 'non-transferable,' and enforce the rule by a black-list for
millions of people. Such a plan would require half the adult
population as clerks and policemen.

And even this would not prevent speculation!

There is no speculation in seats on Chicago elevated trains,
solely because there is no way of buying and reselling the seats.
But it would be impossible to prevent the resale of most things.
Those who bought them at the fixed prices would resell them at
higher prices — as much higher as buyers would pay.

That is why most goods, unlike football tickets, *must* be distributed on the basis of price-bidding.

Who Put Up the Price of Liver?

EVERY consumer who goes to market insists on his inalienable right to select the cut of beef he likes best; but he protests against the high price. Yet he, himself, has made the price, in competition with other buyers who want the same cut.

Who is to get the best cuts?

What price is to be paid?

Here are two ways of asking the same question. Consumers themselves settle the matter by bidding against each other for the same goods. That is why liver used to be one of the cheapest of foods. That is why it is far from cheap now.

In a few cases price-bidding of this kind has been abolished. If a man orders a telephone, he takes what is given him at the established price. If he has his house piped for water, he pays the same rate that his neighbor pays. He cannot get better service by bidding up the price.

If he burns gas, he burns what comes through the main, exactly what all his fellow townsmen burn, and at the same price. He has no choice — *if* he burns gas. But, even in this case, he can affect the price by using a substitute.

The point is that competition in such public services cannot be allowed. There are reasons — reasons which do not apply to the services of dressmakers, steeplejacks, and portrait painters. Unrestricted competition among utilities that must use the public highways would be too annoying and too wasteful.

Ordinary markets, however, are much like auction sales. The successful bidders make the prices and take away the goods. They it is, and only they, who in recent years have put up the price of liver.

Smashing the Thermometer

IN times of inflation, money is produced much faster than goods. Then prices are sure to rise, and people are sure to complain.

But prices are not a cause of trouble. They are a measure of trouble. The people of Ohio did not find fault with the rod which measured the rising waters at Dayton. They protected the city from floods by going back to the source of trouble, and providing an even flow of water. The way to prevent rising prices is to provide for an even flow of goods to market and a flow of money to consumers which increases no more rapidly than the flow of goods.

When we condemn merchants as a class for the prices they charge, or household servants for the wages they demand, we are attacking signs. We might as well try to reduce the temperature by smashing the thermometer.

Every little while somebody introduces a bill in Congress aimed to standardize wages, or to prescribe interest rates, or to prosecute the 'profiteers.' These are all misguided efforts. As a rule, 'profiteers' do not make high prices: high prices make 'profiteers.' And buyers make the high prices by competing with each other for the same goods.

An American salesman in China journeyed by automobile to a village in the interior. A local potentate, spying the strange chariot outside a shop, straightway got in and tried to make it go. When the salesman came out, he found the prince's retinue doing their best to get action. They were belaboring the stubborn car with sticks to drive the devil out.

There is no use trying to get ahead, in China or elsewhere, by flogging non-existent devils. Except in cases of monopoly, there is no use trying to reduce the real cost of living by attacking prices.

'All the Traffic Will Bear'

UNDER the established price and profit system, goods *must* be distributed on the basis of price bidding.

'That may be true,' comes the objection, 'but under such a system, profit-seekers charge all the traffic will bear.'

They certainly do, as a rule. This, however, is merely saying that they charge whatever consumers, competing for the same goods, allow them to charge. And there is no other way of determining who is to get the goods.

But if this is what we mean by profiteering, who shall cast the first stone? Society is based on the expectation that every member will obtain whatever he can for whatever he has to sell. And he rarely disappoints us. Farmer, grocer, meat-packer, preacher, movie star, all our fellow workers in every career known to the Census, including those who are loudest in condemnation of 'profiteers,' usually accept for the commodities and services they wish to sell as much as they can get. When any one declines to do so, his conduct is so exceptional that it figures in the headlines. It has more news value than a man biting a dog.

But until we find a workable substitute for the profit incentive, it is not clear why we should condemn any profit-seeker for doing what society, as a going concern, requires that virtually everybody must do. Moreover, this primitive human trait is not altogether bad. It accounts largely for the progress which the race has made toward higher standards of living.

To many men, this may sound heartless. But any one who understands the functions of price and profit will see that this is all consistent with high ideals. In the interest of human welfare generally, it is important for us all to understand that certain economic laws are neither moral nor immoral. They are inexorable.

Economic Laws Are Not Policemen

ALL along we have been speaking only of main tendencies. We have left out many exceptions to the rules.

Some sellers, for example, in deference to public opinion, or with a view to long-run profits, do not accept as high prices as they can get. Some sellers accept less in order that the field will not be too attractive to newcomers.

Furthermore, we have not discussed cases of monopoly in which prices do not fulfill their economic function. In the case of a monopoly, the competition of buyers for goods does not meet the competition of producers for customers. Therefore, the efforts of consumers to obtain goods, while they tend to drive up prices, do not always bring about increased production of these goods and consequent reduction of prices.

Again, it sometimes happens that a producer who has no competitors—or no competitors who must be considered—can increase his profits by limiting his own output. Competition among buyers of aluminum, for example, does not affect the supply, as does competition for a commodity like cotton cloth that can be freely produced. Consequently, prices of monopoly-controlled commodities may move goods, but without the effects that follow when the volume of production is controlled by the competition of buyers.

The building industry is another case in point. Investigations of that industry show that consumers' desires concerning volume and quality are sometimes frustrated when groups of producers get together to eliminate competition.

So there must be government regulation of monopolies.

Furthermore, however inexorable economic law may be, it does not take effect instantaneously. 'It is not a policeman arresting a criminal the moment he finds him committing a crime. It is a potter gradually shaping a plastic material to his will.'

Every Day is Election Day

WHAT is to be produced to-morrow is decided almost entirely by those who spend money to-day. That is a democratic method. Every citizen has a vote every time he makes a purchase. No one is disfranchised on account of age, sex, race, religion, education, or failure to register.

Every day is election day. Every vote counts: no minority is too small to influence producers. The buyer casts his vote wherever he spends money. The votes are counted promptly and with few errors. The cash register is more dependable than the ballot-box. Those in charge of the polls — business men, all — are dependable, too. It pays.

Still, the result is not ideal; for those consumers who have a lot of money to spend cast too many votes. As a result, human labor is not so directed as to yield the largest possible amount of human happiness. That, however, is not because production is governed by dollar votes. It is because the dollars are not well distributed among the voters.

If the dollars were evenly distributed, still every man would insist on freedom of choice in the markets; and still the most effective way of registering his choice would be by balloting in the market-place, just as he ballots to-day. Slow and bungling would be the efforts to please him of political directors of production.

Our established price and profit system gives the individual citizen more control over business than he has over government. Infrequent, indirect, and uncertain are the ways open to him for expressing his political desires. Many a time his vote at the polls is far from being an effective demand. Sometimes he does not get what he votes for, even when he votes with the majority. His vote in the markets, on the other hand, is almost always effective, for only those producers who heed it promptly are allowed to stay in business.

You Make What You Buy

WHAT you buy to-day, and the prices you pay, are orders for future production. Leave them alone and they'll come home, bringing the goods behind them.

The consumer is in full charge of production schedules. The producer has little real choice. He *has* to make what people decide to buy, or go out of business.

To be sure, one book publisher proudly announces that he is in business, not to make money, but to spread the habit of reading good books. In other words, his mission in life is to decide what is good for people. But if that is what he really means, he is not in business at all. He is in philanthropy. He can keep on indulging himself in that pleasant pursuit only as long as his money lasts. For his enterprise is sterile: it has no powers of reproduction.

The output of our printing-presses, as well as the output of all our other industrial machinery, is decided, not by philanthropists, but by the wishes of people who spend money. They express their wishes — cast their dollar votes in the markets, so to speak — by the very act of spending their money.

The most powerful corporations are not exceptions to the rule. Even the United States Steel Corporation must heed, from day to day, the votes of the buyers. It has no more to say about what it will produce than the village blacksmith.

Do consumers really want to put an end to the production of stupid motion pictures? Or headache powders? Or ugly bill boards? Or high-heeled shoes? Or vile newspapers? Or goods made by child-labor?

Well, they know exactly how to do it! These things will not be *produced* to-morrow unless they are *bought* to-day.

Consumers make what they buy.

Should Speculators be Spanked?

DIFFERENCE of opinion not only makes horse races; it also makes speculators. That is why the Federal Reserve Board cannot prevent speculation. Wherever there is a market in anything — from hay to hogs — there is difference of opinion as to which way prices will move. And so there is speculation. Whichever way the market moves, there is speculation. Whenever there is an unusual rise or fall in prices, there is unusual speculation. As a matter of fact, speculation always has thrived on investment as barnacles grow on ships.

When the bulls are having their way in the stock market, everybody seems to be looking for tips. Between floors, the elevator boy listens. Between sales, the shop girl asks advice. Between shines, Tony puzzles over the *Wall Street News*. Everybody seems to be reaching for a lucky strike in the stock market, instead of appreciating the sweet uses of adversity.

What a loss! So many persons neglecting their business; so many learning to rely on luck; so many losing the back-log of savings. Much of this speculation is indefensible.

Yet there is something to be said for us, reckless though we are. We *all* want to share in the prosperity of our country. That is a natural desire, a worthy ambition. And we have found out that one of the surest ways to achieve that ambition is through part ownership in American business.

Do not tell us to put all our savings in savings banks. Teach us how to invest safely in a wide range of common stocks, representing the soundest concerns in essential industries — a cross section of this prosperity that we read about every day. Show us that this pays and following tips does not. If we are to grow up from wild speculators into wise investors, we need to be educated, not spanked.

New Methods of Financing Business

IN the past decade, American business men discovered a new way of financing business; or, rather, they found new possibilities in an old way. Thousands of corporations, including most of the large ones, reduced their bank loans and bonded indebtedness, and in their place obtained funds through the sale of stocks. Thus they obtained money from the *owners* of the business — the stockholders — instead of from *creditors*.

That is the most notable change in methods of finance since the War. It strengthened the industry of the entire country, for it is sounder business to operate on capital than on debts. A concern which is financed mainly by the sale of stocks is in no danger of being forced, even though solvent, into the hands of creditors. It has a chance to work itself out of temporary troubles. This is better than to have the owners squeezed out by banks or bondholders, and to have somebody who knows nothing about the business trying to run it. It is better both for investors and for the public.

A concern financed by the sale of stocks can go ahead with greater confidence, planning for long-range efficiency, utilizing new inventions, employing more men, paying higher wages, reducing unit costs and prices; doing, in short, what Henry Ford has done. He has always run his business, not on debts, but on capital.

Moreover, a concern financed in this way is in a position to build new equipment and employ more men, precisely when the whole country needs growth of that kind; namely, when a business depression is setting in.

The extraordinary prosperity of American business in 1928 and the confidence in the immediate future were based in part upon this change from debts to stocks.

Stock Speculation and Business

D ID stock speculation hurt business in 1928 and early 1929? It hurt some people, no doubt — swept away their savings, kept their minds from their jobs, led them to depend on luck. But the Reserve Board was not set up to regulate morals, and quite properly did not try to do so. The Board objected to speculation because it 'diverted money from business.'

Was the injury to business revealed by business indexes? The most reliable of these are pig-iron and steel output, freight-car loadings, volume of production, profits, sales to consumers, and real wages. But all these indexes showed vigorous growth of business during the very period when, it was said, business 'suffered.'

To be sure, an old economic theory, still widely taught, regards money as a *fund*. According to this theory, money is literally 'sunk' in a given enterprise, as though it were dropped into a deep well and left there. But money is not a *fund*. It is a *flow*. That part which is used to buy stocks is not sunk in a well. It becomes part of an endless stream. It flows on.

Part of it is used to buy newly issued stocks and bonds. Most of that money flows directly into business, to employ men to build new factories, construct bridges, extend railroad lines, develop water power, and so on. Still another part of the money becomes profits; and part of this money is spent for consumers' goods. That is equally true of the money which is received and spent by hordes of workers who, directly or indirectly, gain their living through selling securities. A still larger part of the money which is received by sellers of stocks is at once deposited in banks, or used to pay bank loans. That, also, is immediately available for business.

Money used to buy stocks is not diverted *from* business. Most of it is directed *into* business.

Saving on the Instalment Plan

NOT only consumer spending but also consumer saving has been aided by instalment plans. During the past decade, several millions of wage-earners, buying shares on partial payments, have become stockholders in the concerns for which they work.

So far-reaching in its effects is this movement that a Harvard professor of economics has called it 'The Present Economic Revolution in the United States.' It is not a *revolution*, but an *evolution* — slow, orderly, and still going on. It is one of those means of distributing prosperity — of giving wage-earners a stake in business stability — which help to *forestall* revolution.

Experience proves, moreover, that lending money on stock collateral to a man who has a steady job, and who buys stock with the intention of paying for it out of earnings, is sound credit policy.

For the most part, these millions of wage-earners have been enabled to buy stocks on instalments, only because the stocks themselves have in some way been used as collateral for bank loans. Thus many small investors, as well as large investors, have made gains before they have fully paid for their shares.

To put a stop to such buying of stocks is to place at a disadvantage every workman of assured earning capacity who desires to share in the growth of the very concern for which he himself is partly responsible.

To deny such opportunities to wage-earners is to enable the rich to acquire even larger shares than they can now acquire in our expanding wealth; for it is a fact that the wealthiest individuals and corporations can borrow money without any collateral at all.

Why Do We Lay Off Workers?

WHY was the basic output of goods in 1921 twenty per cent below the output of 1918? Why was the volume of business early in 1930 over ten per cent below normal? Why do we *ever* curtail production in general, bank furnaces, shut down mills, throw men out of work? For one reason, and one only. Because we cannot sell our goods to the people who want to use them at prices which make continued production possible.

The reason we cannot sell as much as we can make seems plain enough to the plain people. It is because they cannot buy so much. And the reason they cannot buy so much is because they lack the money. It is not because they refuse to buy. There was no consumers' strike in 1921; no such thing in 1930. There is never a consumers' strike.

The one thing that is needed, above all others, to sustain a forward movement of business is enough money in the hands of consumers. Let it be known that there will be buyers for any producible goods, and the goods will be produced. Lack of markets is the only reason why the General Electric Company does not turn out more lamps: the only reason why the Thor Company does not make more washing-machines. Nothing else stops the Sherwin-Williams Company from making more paint.

If any one appeared in Chicago any day with plenty of cash or credit, and an order for almost anything — say, a thousand pairs of silk knee-breeches with diamond buckles — the order would be filled promptly. It would be just as easy to have a thousand whaling vessels launched on Lake Michigan. See that consumers have the money, and organized business will look out for the rest. There will be no shortage of money on the producing side. A willing buyer does not have to wait long; but a willing seller may have to wait forever.

'Good Times' and 'Bad Times'

THERE are 'good times' and 'bad times.' Everybody knows that. Everybody knows, too, that even in 'good times,' some lines of business suffer.

Even in 'good times,' there may be *relative* overproduction. There may be too much cotton cloth, in relation to the demand for cotton cloth; or too many potatoes, in relation to the demand for potatoes. Not to mention too many flesh-colored stockings produced just before they go out of style; or too many radio sets produced just before better ones come upon the market. Overproduction of that kind cannot be prevented, as long as producers are free to make mistakes, and consumers are free to change their minds.

But the *relative* overproduction of cotton cloth, or potatoes, or anything else, cannot bring 'good times' to an end, if there is no *general* overproduction; that is to say, if there are enough buyers of goods, taken as a whole, to keep up the general level of prices.

For several years before the stock market collapse of 1929, we had 'good times'; very good, indeed, compared with the general-overproduction period of 1920–21. For there was an unusually steady increase of output, sales, real wages, and profits, without any marked change in the price-level, or any considerable piling up of unsold goods.

As long as we thus prevent general overproduction, we prevent business depressions. But there is no way to do that except by seeing to it that the flow of consumer income keeps pace with the flow of commodities.

If we can sustain the flow of income at the right rate, we can have 'good times' all the time.

The Buyer Rings the Bell

BUSINESS waiting for a buyer is like an engine house waiting for a fire alarm. Some of the firemen are playing checkers; some are tipped back against the wall, yawning.

Suddenly the fire bell rings. Instantly every one is on his feet.

In the world of business a buyer can ring the bell at any time, and nobody else can. Let a buyer sound the alarm, and sellers will rush after him like firemen to a fire.

You, for example, want to buy a hat. You step into a shop. At once every idle salesman is alert, expectant, 'rearin' to go.' That is what buyers mean to the industrial world.

Once buyers flock into the shops and throw their money down on the counters, the clinking of the coins is heard far and near. The shopkeepers hear the merry music first and broadcast. There is never enough static in the air to prevent dealers from hearing that tune. The jobbers, as soon as they hear it, send larger orders to the wholesalers. Then the wholesalers, not to be caught napping, increase their orders to the manufacturers. Whereupon the manufacturers take on more workers, order more copper and cotton, more lumber and lathes, more tin and turbines. All of which induces the miners to dig more ore, the farmers to plant more cotton, the lumbermen to fell more trees.

Thus here, there, and everywhere, employers find courage and the unemployed find jobs.

The important thing to remember is how the whole process gets started. It is set in motion by people who spend money. When there are enough of them, in enough stores, buying enough things, business is prosperous — inevitably — all the way from the retailer to the rancher, no matter what else happens.

Business is always 'rearin' to go.' It is always ready to plunge ahead. But only the buyer can ring the bell.

What Makes Good Business?

WHAT makes good business? Ask ten business men, and the chances are that at least nine will answer, 'Enough buying by consumers.'

What else *is* needed? Nothing else. Adequate consumer demand is all that business requires.

Take your own case, for example. You are, let us say, a manufacturer of chairs. What conditions do you consider necessary for your success? Do you ask society to protect you against changes in style, or against the efficiency of your competitors? You do not.

Do you expect to have a law passed that will require consumers to use up more chairs? You certainly do not.

Do you think that the Government should regulate the wages which you and your competitors pay, or the prices which you receive? Far from it. You know that you must meet all such risks and take your chances, just as long as consumers are free to buy what they please, and you and all other men are free to compete for their dollars. In the face of these risks, moreover, you are confident that you can take care of yourself.

What you *do* ask, and reasonably, is protection against a slump in the buying power of consumers as a whole; such a slump, for instance, as came in 1921, when the income of consumers fell off nine billion dollars. Or even the slump which followed the 1929 collapse of stock prices, when volume of trade, taken as a whole, fell nearly 20 per cent. From a catastrophe of this sort, virtually every business man suffers, regardless of his efficiency.

You *do* ask, and reasonably, that society — which has devised its own monetary system and has absolute control over it — shall see to it that consumers receive enough money, week in and week out, to prevent a collapse of business as a whole.

Sunshine Cure for Tired Business

OPTIMISM alone does not open up blast furnaces or take men out of the bread lines. It does not put a single dollar into pay envelopes, or take a single car off the dealers' hands.

Sunshine may cure a wasting condition of the human body; but it cannot cure a wasting condition of the body politic. A self-starter may save time in starting an engine, but only a steady supply of fuel can keep it running. Sunshine campaigns may help to get business under way, but only a steady supply of consumers' dollars can keep business going.

When the income of consumers falls off, their buying falls off, no matter how many Pollyannas there are abroad in the land, who insist that 'business is fundamentally sound, and credit plentiful.' No amount of cheerful talk can sustain wages if the total volume of money in circulation is falling off rapidly. Nothing could restore business to the high general level of the first half of 1929, until a billion dollars and more of money that went out of circulation with the crash of the stock market was put back into circulation.

For a large part of the bank credit which was based on stock collateral, and first used to buy stocks, flowed on through all the channels of business. There is no other way of accounting for the fact that the volume of production and the volume of bank loans, for two years before the stock market crash, increased at almost the same rate.

President Hoover and his advisers understood that. They did not hold conferences for the purpose of issuing optimistic bulletins. They insisted that wage rates be maintained, and the one act of Henry Ford, in announcing a raise of wages as he left the White House, was worth more to business than a thousand sunshine talks.

General Overproduction

ACCORDING to an old economic theory, still widely accepted, general overproduction is impossible.

'How absurd it is' — so runs the argument — 'to suppose that the supply of goods can ever be greater than the demand. Demand and supply are the same thing. One man's supply is another man's demand. For example, when Sam Witham drives to town with a load of hay, the hay is his demand for goods and another man's supply of goods. Sam has added to demand, and also to supply, exactly one load of hay. The balance between supply and demand remains perfect.

'To be sure, Sam may sell the hay for money, and spend the money for a harness. But money is a mere medium of exchange. Nothing matters except the goods. Sam disposed of a load of hay: he acquired a harness.

'True, he may find too much hay in the market, whereas harnesses may be comparatively scarce. In that case, there is *relative* overproduction of hay. But, of course, not all goods can be *relatively* overproduced. So there can be no such thing as *general* overproduction.'

That is the old argument. It is false because it confines its attention to goods. It ignores the part which money plays.

Of course *general* overproduction would be impossible, if there were no money — if goods were exchanged only for goods. In that case the old argument would be sound. But who trades by barter? Scarcely anybody.

Now the moment we consider what may happen to money, we see at once that there may readily be general overproduction of goods, in relation to the money which consumers offer in exchange for goods. As a matter of fact, every business depression is marked by that kind of overproduction.

The Next World War

THE greatest economic need is a flow of money to consumers which keeps pace with the flow of finished goods. With such incomes, consumers could buy all that was produced at prices — on the average — sufficient to make continued production profitable. The certainty that they could do so would be enough to induce both employers and employees to increase output, for the very good reason that higher real wages and higher real profits would depend mainly on increased output.

If, to the efficient system which now provides money for production, we could add an equally efficient means of providing money for consumption, we could make sustained progress toward realizing the potential output of industry; greater progress, therefore, toward higher standards of living.

Adequate, sustained consumer-demand would do more than anything else within human control toward abolishing poverty, maintaining employment, increasing good-will among men, and maintaining the peace of the world.

No other means of preventing war, now that we have the Kellogg Peace Pact, holds out such large possibilities as this. The World War was in large part a struggle for *outside* markets among industrial nations which had found no means of giving their *own* ill-nourished, ill-clad, ill-housed people enough money to buy what they themselves could produce. The same difficulty was a major cause of the destructive competition, after the War, in building tariff walls.

It is, therefore, difficult to exaggerate the importance of sustaining the flow of money to the people at the right rate. The next World War, if it does come, may well be the last war — at least the last war in which the present great nations will have any interest, for it may well destroy civilization itself.

Consumption Regulates Production

WHAT do we mean by production? For our purposes, we mean the turning-out of things which are ready for final use; not lathes, and harvesters, and spindles, which are used up in the process of making other things, but chairs, and bread, and shirts — the things, in general, for which wages are spent. These are called consumers' goods; and consumption is the process of using them up.

Now consumption is the final end of our whole complex, industrial world. Shoes are not made to stock shops, nor leather to lie in warehouses, nor gowns to decorate store windows. These myriads of toilers, going daily to their work — as long as there is work to be had — planting corn, painting cars, trimming hats — what are they all about? The one end of all their efforts is the consumption by somebody of whatever they can produce. All other aims are incidental.

Since, therefore, the final end of all economic activity is consumption, and since it is possible to produce far more than we consume, *consumption regulates production.*

There is no use building more wooden ships when hundreds are lying idle at the wharves; no use operating all our textile mills and tanneries at capacity when it is not possible to sell the cloth and the leather which we have already produced. ·

Too commonplace to mention, this fact may seem; yet it is the basic fact in the whole economic problem. There could not be a serious setback of business in general if consumption regularly kept pace with production. Sustained business-depression accompanied by adequate consumer-demand is no more possible than drought accompanied by heavy rains.

In this money and profit world in which we have to do business — the only one, by the way, which has ever proved workable on a large scale — sales regulate consumption, and consumption regulates production.

The Robot-Consumer

A ROBOT chemist, with an electric eye, radio brains, and magnet hands, now functions without human supervision. Here, at last, except for a gadget or two, is the creature described, but never produced, by some of the old economists. We refer to the Robot-Consumer; the one who, it was said, automatically appeared with a five-dollar bill in his hand, every time a factory turned out a five-dollar pair of shoes. In that way, we used to be assured, production automatically finances consumption.

A robot chemist, gravely preparing synthetic paregoric for a self-winding baby, would make an interesting museum piece. But it would have no immediate effect on the volume of trade. An adequate Robot-Consumer would. It would once and for all dispose of the vexatious problem of 'over-production' and 'underconsumption' — two names for one thing.

When this Robot-Consumer is perfected, production really will regulate consumption. The Robot-Consumer will be geared to take away all the products of industry. Everybody will have a job who wants one, and the millennium will be seen with the naked eye.

The perfected Robot-Consumer will have to have, in addition to an electric eye, radio brains, and magnet hands, an automatically increasing income and a self-dispensing bank roll. Inventors can no doubt work out these minor details.

In the meantime, the only way we can gear human consumers to take away all the products of industry is by providing them with enough purchasing power. This is industry's chief problem to-day. This takes human supervision and a lot of it.

We cannot achieve that end by shutting our eyes to the facts and repeating the old saw, 'Production automatically finances consumption.'

It doesn't.

'There Ought to be a Law'

THERE ought to be a law against talking movies. They are throwing men out of work; girls, too, as Hollywood bears noisy testimony. There ought to be a law against improved shoe machinery. Too many shoe workers are out of work already. There ought to be a law against dial telephones. There ought to be a law against —

But we cannot outlaw all labor-saving devices. Even if we spent all our time making laws, we could not keep up with inventors. Nobody knows where they will break out next with a device which makes two men idle where only one was idle before. Yesterday it was in the cotton mills. To-day it is in the paint shops. To-morrow it may be almost anywhere.

For centuries the world has been trying in vain to stop these scientists — ridiculing them, excommunicating them, exiling them, burning them at the stake. The author of Ecclesiastes even tried to end their troublesome activities by writing poetry about them. 'This only have I found,' he sang sadly; 'that God made men upright; but they have sought out many inventions.'

After all, there is something to be said for these scientists. They have brought within the reach of the common people of to-day more comfort and security and health and music than kings and queens enjoyed a few generations ago.

Back in the sixteenth century, such men as Copernicus, Kepler, and Galileo ran clear by all the 'stop' signals of their day. Somebody had to do that before there could be any telephones, or radios, or airplanes. Somebody had to ignore the plight of the poor copyist before there could be any printing-presses.

Yes, there ought to be a law. And there *is* a law. Here it is: The surest way to keep down wages is to keep down scientists.

Gold in Test-Tubes

W HAT is the greatest contribution which chemistry has made to the world in the last hundred years?' asked an examination paper.

'Blondes,' wrote a resourceful student.

His only error was in getting his consonants mixed. Chemistry's greatest contribution has not been dye-products, but by-products.

Here is the latest news from the research-front: Farmers may soon build straw houses; that is, houses made of synthetic lumber, compounded of straw. It may still be true that we cannot make bricks without straw. But soon we shall make houses without bricks — if we have plenty of straw.

The bespectacled chemist, messing about in the laboratory, is industry's great white hope. At any moment, he may hit on a profitable use for mountains of waste. He may turn goldenrod into rubber, as well as cornhusks into silk. He is capable of challenging even the pig's squeal as a symbol of waste's irreducible minimum.

Any day, out of the chemist's patient messing, may spring forth the combination which will lift a whole industry from 'hard sledding' to prosperity. Any day, too, he may make a discovery which will create an entirely new industry; and it is only through such discoveries that we have made as much progress as we have made, in this generation, toward more of the good things of life for more people. The Du Pont laboratories, for example, have shown the world, year after year, how to create entirely new products.

All through the ages, chemists have tried to find out how to turn the baser metals into gold. They may never find out. There may be no such thing as the philosopher's stone. Still, in a very real sense, 'Thar's gold in them thar test-tubes.'

Plowing With Buffaloes

NO one knows what poverty is until he sees the great American family with only one car. We laugh at that, because the average American family already has one car, and sees no reason why it should not aspire to two.

How has the American family achieved this standard of living? There is a picturesque answer to this question on the Island of Oahu, in the Hawaiian group.

On one side of this Island, brown-skinned, nearly naked men go forth in search of food, as did their ancestors a century ago. They wade into the ocean and fish with nets and spears. They cultivate little patches of land with primitive tools and water buffaloes. And if, by happy chance, they have a surplus of fresh food, they have no means of keeping it fresh.

On the other side of the Island, the cannery of the Hawaiian Pineapple Company, started a generation ago by a young man from Boston who was homesteading a small tract of land, now puts up 68 million cans per year. A single machine labels 500 cans per minute. The fruit is raised on land which was thrown up from the bottom of the ocean by volcanoes, thousands of years ago, and remained of no use to man until Science and the Planters went into business together. As a result of this partnership, every plantation and every laborer is enabled, year after year, to produce a better product and more of it, and to preserve it for use all over the world.

Thus a little volcanic island in the middle of the Pacific Ocean tells the story of the economic progress of the United States. Look on this picture, and then on that:

The native, trudging after his crude plow and his leisurely water buffalo on his little plot of land.

The modern cannery, packing the product of 38,000 acres, at the rate of over a million cans per week.

Science as a Pace-Maker

BENJAMIN FRANKLIN, preacher of common sense, was so far-visioned a dreamer as to send a kite into the sky to bring down lightning. Yet, if he could return to us to-day, he would be overcome with astonishment.

In place of the Leyden jar, he would find a thirty million horse-power generator. In place of the ten weeks' packet on which he sailed to England, he would find a fifty-thousand-ton ocean liner, oil-fired, and turbine driven. The very air he breathed would be reduced before his eyes to a liquid, boiling on a cake of ice. He would learn of soil analysis, seed selection, fertilizers plucked from the thin air, a harvesting machine doing the work of fifty men, and countless other ways of making two — or even a dozen — calories of food grow where one grew before. He would find men making leather, silk, dyes — almost anything — out of materials which we used to throw away.

The new uses of wood products are such, says Dr. Harrison E. Howe, 'that the poor fiber never knows, nowadays, whether it is destined to become literature or lingerie.'

We know how to make synthetic dishes, furniture, clothes, foods, even houses and coal. We know how to make better machines out of newly discovered alloys; how to save water power now going to waste; how to electrify our railroads; how to bring water to remote farms.

So great are all these gains in productive power that business, in this country at least, seems to have almost within its grasp the means of abolishing poverty. Yet now, as in the past, our use of better methods and machines lags far behind our ability to invent them. Economists and business men do not keep up with chemists and physicists.

Why Labor Fears Science

NOT long ago, seventy-five telephone operators in Butte, Montana, took off their occupational millinery for the last time. Butte had 'gone dial.' Every one was happy, except the seventy-five girls who had lost the only jobs for which they had been trained. These girls had been sacrificed, as one of them ruefully said, 'to the little Moloch of dials and numerals, twisting so satisfactorily under the Mayor's forefinger.' It was another triumph of Science — another tragedy for a group of skilled laborers.

No wonder Labor fears Science. Science is cold, impersonal, ruthless. The truth is the truth and must be discovered at all costs. Science cares not what the costs are, or who pays them.

The replacing of telephone operators by dials is scientific progress. Large numbers of workers are thereby released for other work.

'Other work!' But where is other work to be found? That, too, is a problem for Science to solve.

For the most part, Science has always proved equal to the task. It has given rise to new industries which have provided jobs for most of the displaced workers. The invention of the automobile alone created at least four million new jobs. The lot of Labor, as a whole, has been greatly improved by Science.

But usually there is a lag between the losing of one job and the finding of another. Worse still, some of the displaced workers are too old ever to acquire new skills. On them the cost of scientific progress falls too heavily.

That is *Industry's* problem. Science will go right ahead making progress; but Industry must see to it that there are no human victims of progress. When Industry has solved that problem, Labor will no longer fear Science.

'What Hast Thou in the House?'

ONE of the earliest exponents of scientific research as a help in abolishing poverty was a man named Elisha. When a destitute widow implored his help, he presented her with the most fundamental questionnaire ever compiled by a social welfare worker. He inquired, gently, 'What hast thou in the house?'

When she told him of her sole meager possession — a small cruse of oil — he gave her practical advice: he told her how to use what she had, so that what she had would be enough.

Scientists are constantly showing us how to make use of what we have; not only the millions of cruses of oil that lie hidden in the bowels of the earth, but as well the millions of horse power that needlessly run to waste in our rivers. Recently came the announcement by the United States Bureau of Standards of a new formula for sugar — sugar made, if you please, from strawstacks, cotton seeds, shrubs, and what not, at a cost of five cents a pound. As a matter of fact, the chief business of science is the discovery of wealth which has always been 'in the house,' but which has always been overlooked.

Material progress, after all, is only the discovery by science of more and more of the good things we 'have in the house,' and the distribution by industry of more and more of these things to more and more persons. 'The tiring discussions of politics seem to be our guide,' said Pasteur, 'but what really leads us forward are a few scientific discoveries and their application.'

There is no known limit to human intelligence; no immediate danger, therefore, of a dearth of the good things we 'have in the house.'

The scientific sons of Elisha are proving it.

'More Pay and Less Work'

NEARLY every morning we see something in the head-lines about the persistent struggle of wage-earners every-where for 'More Pay and Less Work.' Much fault has always been found with organized labor for pursuing that aim. Yet any lower aim is indefensible.

The object in view, needless to say, is not more leisure forced upon jobless men, but more leisure voluntarily chosen as part of the increased rewards of fully employed men. Nor is the aim less work of all kinds, voluntarily undertaken, but less work imposed on the average worker as a condition of survival.

The main fault with this aim is that certain groups of workers have pursued it at the expense of other groups, whereas it should be attained for all workers.

'More Pay and Less Work' cannot be achieved merely by forcing up money wages; or by limiting output; or by increasing the danger of business losses in an already highly precarious profit-seeking world; or by weakening those incentives to pro-ductive activity which are actually operating to-day. For with-out them we could not have made those gains which we un-doubtedly have made in real wages and in leisure.

The latest extension of the Einstein theory, it is true, demon-strates that those things which appear to exist do not exist, and the only reality is that which is unreal. Nevertheless, we still believe that there is no way of enabling people to eat apples which are not grown, or to ride on railroads which have not been built. And we do not see how reducing the hours of labor in itself raises apples, or builds railroads.

But any change whatever in our economic system which re-sults in a larger output for each labor hour can and should re-sult, as well, in 'more pay and less work.'

Why Not Have a Four-Hour Day?

'THE four-hour working day would solve the unemployment problem,' declares George Bernard Shaw. That sounds logical. If the workers now labor eight hours a day, it might take twice as many workers to do the same work in four hours.

But if that is the way to abolish unemployment, why has it not been abolished? A decade or two ago, the ten-hour day and even the twelve-hour day were common. Then came shorter hours; also fewer days per week for most workers. But shortening the hours of labor did not shorten the bread lines.

Shorter hours actually would produce prosperity if shorter hours yielded increased purchasing power at a time when business falters for lack of buyers. But leisure is not legal tender. More leisure we ought to have, but more leisure does not necessarily mean more consumption.

'An extra day of leisure,' says Henry Ford, 'is going to bring large results, for the people will have time to expand their sense of need, and therefore will increase their consumption.' That seems to be a mistaken notion. Wage-earners, as a whole, already have plenty of time in which to spend all the money which they have to spend; and there are already plenty of things which they would like to buy. They cannot buy these things with free time.

Workers with a five-day week will spend more money than workers with a six-day week, if they have more money. Otherwise, they will not. Workers with a six-hour day will spend more money than workers with an eight-hour day, if they have more money. Otherwise, they will not.

A shorter working day may well come as a *reward* for *good* business management. This means gaining ground. But a shorter working day forced upon us as a *penalty* for *bad* management means losing ground.

90

Corner-Store Economics

THEY say that Sam Witham, who has kept the corner store at Sandwich Center going on thirty years, recently had a streak of liberality.

It seems that Joe Turner, who owed a balance of $18 on a mowing machine, which debt he could not pay in cash, offered to settle the account with eggs.

'No,' said Sam, 'I can't accept eggs in payment. But don't let that bother you. Order whatever you like and go ahead running up bills. And if you want to borrow more money, say the word.'

Absurd?

Yes, unbelievable. Everybody knows that Sam Witham — sound, practical man that he is — would not for a minute handle his business that way. If he did, his store would be in the hands of a receiver, and he himself in the hands of a receiver, too, as soon as an asylum could be found to receive him.

Yet Sam Witham, as a citizen of the United States, together with all his fellow citizens, is conducting international trade in some such way. For it is a fact that our foreign debtors cannot fully pay their debts to us except with goods. It is also a fact that not for a single year, in the past quarter-century, have we made it possible for our foreign debtors to pay their debts with goods. And now we have made it still more difficult by erecting still higher tariff walls.

At the same time, we are constantly granting new loans abroad, thus adding billions to the debts of foreign countries, without having any idea how they will ever be able to pay what they already owe.

How would it do for Congress to send a commission to Sandwich Center to study economics with Sam Witham?

Getting the Other Man's Money

IN the 'Bank Catechism,' published by one of the leading banks of New York City, appears this statement:

'The more we can sell to foreign countries at a profit, the greater becomes the wealth of this country, because we are getting the other man's money.'

This is far from the truth. We cannot add to the wealth of this country by 'getting the other man's money.' It is only by getting the other man's goods that we can profit by selling goods to him. It does not help us much to acquire purchasing power that we are never going to use. It does not help us to increase the debts owed to us, if we are never to allow these debts to be paid.

Yet by means of higher and higher tariffs, we are constantly making it more difficult for the other fellow to pay his debts. We are preventing him from shipping as much to us as we ship to him. We are still in the grip of the old fallacy of a 'favorable' balance of trade. We do not yet understand that the only *really favorable* trade is an equal exchange of goods.

Every nation is pursuing the same stupid policy. Every nation is striving to export more than it imports. This appears to be the only case in history where the people of the world, with one accord, have fully accepted the precept of the Bible, 'It is more blessed to give than to receive.'

Our own forty-eight States, carrying on the internal trade of this country, know that each of them cannot sell to the others more than it buys from the others. But forty-eight nations, carrying on the trade of the world, cannot see that point.

Naturally, the nations of Europe are now planning to put up new trade barriers against the United States, because of the higher rates in our new tariff.

Such rivalry breeds a similar vicious spiral of competition in armaments, and is one of the basic causes of war.

Can You Live on Paris Green?

ANY one who has been hard pressed to support his family will be cheered to learn that the new tariff transfers to the free list women's unembroidered cotton gloves, citron peel, Paris green, and fish scrap unfit for human consumption. If any one can clothe and feed his family with those things, the new tariff will reduce his cost of living. And if the United States increases its consumption of those commodities by several thousand per cent, perhaps European countries can begin paying their debts to us. Apparently the prospect has not cheered Europe.

Still, is there not something to be said in favor of a protective tariff? Certainly there is. But any tariff is unsound which prevents other nations from paying their debts. In the long run, the only 'favorable' balance of trade is an *exact* balance.

A different opinion has just been expressed by one of our bankers. He asserts that the billions which foreign countries owe us can never be paid, but they are nevertheless perfectly sound debts. That seems to be a new principle of finance, and one which has undeniable attractions. Any man who owes this banker money and could use more, should not hesitate to avail himself of the implied offer. Yet something tells us that this open-minded policy applies only to over-seas customers, not to home folks. Still we cannot understand how unsound business becomes sound business merely because the debt is huge and the debtor is far away.

If higher and higher tariffs is Uncle Sam's story, and he continues to stick to it, we see only one way to collect our foreign debts. We shall all have to start wearing women's unembroidered cotton gloves and add a new dish to our diet. We don't pretend it will be pleasant, but what, after all, is a little Paris green, more or less, to a patriot?

Bridges and Politics

HOW long would it take to remove a railroad bridge, covering a span of 182 feet, and replace it with a new one, weighing 560 tons? How long would traffic be suspended?

Two weeks? Two months? What is your guess?

Well, this is what happened on the Pennsylvania Railroad, in a heavy snowstorm, with the mercury showing fifteen degrees of frost. A train appeared through the storm and ran over the old bridge across the Monongahela River at Pittsburgh. Two minutes later the tracks had been carried to a new position. Next, the new 560-ton bridge was swung into place. Five minutes had passed by. Fifteen minutes later the new bridge was ready for use. Not a single train had been delayed.

That is what comes of dealing with scientific matters by scientific methods. It was a problem of measurement, and it was solved by measurement.

No 'interested parties' tried to induce the engineers to cover that 182-foot span with a 90-foot bridge. No vote of Congress was taken to determine whether the hoisting engines were equal to the job.

Economic problems, also, are mainly scientific problems. They are questions of 'how much.' They can be solved by measurements, but not by politics.

The tariff is such a problem. A sound tariff can no more be designed by the counting of votes than can a sound bridge.

A sound tariff would help to bridge over international gulfs, rather than to make gulfs. But to be sound, a tariff must not be based on political guesses as to how much inconvenience international traffic will bear. A tariff, like a bridge, should be designed to facilitate traffic.

What Everybody Knows

HERE is something that everybody knows:

The more use Illinois makes of improved machinery, the more wealth Illinois produces per unit of labor. The more wealth Illinois produces, the greater is her buying power. The greater the buying power of Illinois, the greater is the market for Florida oranges, Michigan furniture, Missouri shoes, and California films. Wage-earners have prospered in Chicago, partly because the automobile industry has prospered in Detroit. Anything that hurts business in Michigan hurts business in Illinois. In short, no part of this country can prosper without helping all other parts. Everybody knows that.

Here, however, is something that everybody does *not* know: What is true of two parts of the same country is true of two different countries. Economic laws are constantly making non-stop flights across international boundaries. Anything that increases the productivity of Europe increases the market for American goods. America can rise to higher standards of living most rapidly, not by keeping European standards down, but by putting them up.

The productivity per worker is about three and one half times as great in this country as it is in Europe. If, through our help, European workers were lifted to our level of efficiency, their buying power might be increased by over seven hundred billion dollars a year. Even if only five per cent of that increased buying power were used to buy the products of the United States, that would enlarge our markets by 50 per cent.

Nothing ever works out with such mathematical precision. Growth in that direction, however, is immediately feasible, and should receive the constant stimulus of our foreign policy.

Your Share of the National Income

WHEN consumers receive enough money to buy the output of industry, they spend it. When they spend enough, industry goes right on producing. Industry is set up for that very purpose.

But sometimes consumers do *not* spend enough. Why?

The trouble, some people say, is not the wrong flow of money, but the flow of money to the wrong people. No use giving more money to the surfeited rich! That will not bring more buyers into the markets.

The fact that some people make millions by speculating in stocks does not enable coal and textile workers to become better customers. No one can deny that. The fact that there are widows who have no money to buy milk for their sick babies, while there are many mothers who could and would buy it at a hundred times the price, is evidence of an unfortunate distribution of wealth. That, too, no one can deny.

A more even distribution of dollar income surely would help to flatten out the peaks and fill in the valleys of business. If wage-earners steadily obtained a larger share of the national dollar income, trade and employment would be better sustained.

And everybody would be happier — including the well-to-do.

That is just what has happened in recent years.

But a wider *distribution* of dollar income is not enough. To increase the food value of a loaf of bread, it is necessary to do more than to cut it into more uniform slices. To increase the buying power of consumers, it is necessary to do more than to distribute the national income more evenly. The *total* dollar income must be larger — constantly larger — in order to keep pace with the growing goods income.

Ford's Folly

IN the industrial history of the twentieth century, two wage decisions will deserve distinction. The first took place in 1914, when Henry Ford astounded the world by announcing that henceforth he would pay a minimum wage of five dollars for an eight-hour day. The second occurred in 1929. It came when business was falling into a decline in spite of frequent hypodermics of optimistic talk. The nation's payroll was falling off. There was danger of a vicious spiral of wage-cutting. In the face of this danger, Henry Ford announced an increase of his minimum wage to seven dollars, and an annual increase of wages of over nineteen million dollars.

The business world did not gasp as it did in 1914, when the five-dollar wage was announced. Then disaster was predicted. 'Ford's Folly' was ridiculed. Even as late as 1921, the business world knew so little about the basis of its own prosperity as to allow wages to fall off seven billion dollars. At that time, meetings of corporation directors usually discussed the question of how wages could be reduced.

Now, hardly anybody ever talks about the desirability of reducing wages. The aim is to reduce unit costs of production *without reducing wages.*

That is to say, without destroying customers.

Reduction of the general level of wages is not a cure for hard times. It does more than anything else to prolong hard times. Employers, in their own interests, should pay as high wages as they can pay, and still expand their business on a sound basis. Mr. Ford is right: 'The best wages that have ever been paid are not nearly as high as they ought to be.'

Does It Pay to Pay High Wages?

HENRY FORD is spending millions in teaching European manufacturers that they cannot afford to pay low wages. Most American manufacturers learned that lesson long ago. They did a lot of complaining, it is true, back in 1914, when Henry Ford established the minimum wage of five dollars a day. They declared that wage-earners would go down-hill to vice and profligacy, and employers would go over the hill to the poorhouse. But after they had exercised their inalienable right of protest, they settled down to the task of enabling their workers to *earn* more money.

The result is summed up in a book called 'Real Wages,' by Paul H. Douglas. Professor Douglas shows that, since 1914, real wages in all manufacturing concerns in the United States have increased 36 per cent. Meantime, American manufacturers as a whole have been more prosperous than any manufacturers have ever been anywhere in the world.

Henry Ford is right. In the United States, at least, it pays to pay high wages.

Nevertheless, employers in Cork and Copenhagen are now complaining, just as employers in Detroit complained in 1914, that Ford wages are too high. The minimum wage in the Ford tractor plant in Cork is the highest in Ireland. Ford wages in Copenhagen are about twice as high, and in Italy three times as high, as the wages for similar work in other factories.

Does it pay to pay such high wages in Europe? It certainly does, according to the report of the European Ford Company. In Denmark, where the Company pays the highest wages, the costs are lowest. In Belgium, where the wages are lowest, the costs are highest.

There is only one way to teach Europe that it pays to pay high wages. Henry Ford has chosen that way.

Blood-Letting Doctors

THE economic Doctors of Despair have their most doleful bedside manner. Commercially, they say, the country has been on a spree. There must be a letting of blood. Wages and prices must be further reduced.

In unison, the Doctors chant: 'To every action, there *must* be an equal and opposite reaction; and we have not yet had reaction enough.'

What is enough? Already, in one short year, we have gone back to the Pre-World War level of prices. How much further back must we go?

The level of prices is determined almost entirely by the level of wages; and both are almost entirely subject to human control. There is no scientific basis whatever for making a law of *prices* out of a law of *physics*.

It may be that the declining rate of gold production will force the world to accept a long period of slowly declining prices. We do not think so. Ways have been found in t'e past of making a given volume of gold support a larger volume of money. Other ways can be found in the future.

In any event, a decline in prices, over the next twenty years, having to do solely with the world's stock of monetary gold, is nothing for the Doctors of Despair to shake their heads over. Such a decline would be too gradual to send the patient to the hospital.

The Doleful Doctors demand more than that. They want to operate at once. The deeper the wage-cuts, the better. The life-blood of the body economic must be drawn.

The blood-letting Medical Doctors of the age of ignorance and superstition are now forbidden to practice.

The blood-letting Economic Doctors are still at large.

Are High Wages All We Need?

NO matter how high the plunger pushes the floor of the elevator, it pushes the ceiling higher still. Everybody knows that.

Wages and prices are like the floor and the ceiling of an elevator. They move together, one always above the other — as long as business prospers, as long as producers get enough for their product to enable them to keep on producing it.

The wages paid for producing a shirt cannot catch up with the price of the shirt, any more than the floor can catch up with the ceiling. For the price of the shirt covers wages *and* other costs, *plus* the profits. Otherwise, no one could possibly keep on making shirts very long, unless he had the means of running a philanthropic factory.

As there must be a space between the floor and the ceiling of the elevator in order to permit standing room and air for passengers, so there must be a profit interval between wages and prices in order to provide standing room and the breath of life to business. That is why high wages, alone, cannot solve the problem of unemployment.

Every wage-earner can see what the trouble is. He knows that he can lift a jack under his car, notch by notch. He also knows that no matter how high he lifts the jack, the car goes higher still.

Now the price of any product, and the wages that are paid in producing it, must remain in the relation of the car and the jack. Otherwise, business cannot prosper. Consequently, putting up wages in Ford factories and all other *existing* factories cannot yield consumers enough to buy the products of those factories. There must *also* be increased expenditures, at the right rate, for *new* private capital and *new* public works.

We need high wages, but high wages are not all we need.

Is a Million a Year High Wages?

NOTHING is necessarily better because it is bigger. Not even wages. A medium-sized salary, that settles like a homing pigeon into the pocket every Saturday night, is mightier than a big hourly wage that drops in for only an occasional visit and then, without warning, disappears for weeks at a time.

The man who signs a yearly contract, carrying with it sufficient salary to see his family through everything but an epidemic, smiles bitterly when the mechanics' hourly wages are mentioned. Quickly he computes the sum this 'bandit' earns in a year. Isn't it colossal?

It might be if he had a chance to earn it.

There is the rub. It is an exceptional skyscraper job that provides the mechanic with work for more than six weeks at a time. Two is nearer the average. Then school is out, and the mechanic skips gaily forth to devote his care-free, high-priced hours to finding another job.

Budgeting, which has upset digestions even in homes run on a yearly income basis, must be a riot in a mechanic's ménage. There is no system of accounting nimble enough to enable a mechanic's wife to plan the orderly expenditure of an income that comes loping in with eighty dollars one week, playfully drops to twenty dollars the second, and doesn't take the trouble to come around at all for the next three.

A mechanic, congratulated once too often on his estimated earnings, replied tersely: 'Yes, a million dollars a year would be high wages, but it wouldn't mean much if you were fired at the end of the first minute.'

Best in the long run is the job that runs long. Fortunately for all of us, the building industry is constantly finding new ways of making jobs run longer.

'To Have and to Hold'

ONCE upon a time, when Industry was a man making by hand a pair of shoes, the only person who could fire a worker was himself. If he made good shoes, he was in no danger of being 'let out.' If he didn't make good shoes, he just naturally fell out.

A manufacturer, in those pre-hysteric days, profited only from his own labor. He suffered only from his own laziness. Nobody but his family was dependent on his ability. He had no duty to any worker but himself. Outside of such obligation to his stomach as he chose to recognize, he could keep his 'plant' going or not, as he pleased.

Industry to-day has far different responsibilities. It *does* profit by the labor of others. It has a duty to these others. It must find a way to keep going.

Industry must increase its out-lets.

Industry must decrease its let-outs.

The scenario of American Industry is thrilling. All it needs is better continuity. Once industrial leaders accept the responsibility for providing this continuity, they will re-write the scenario, introducing longer and better situations.

Here and there, employers are doing just that. They are developing Business Consecutives — men who can look a pay-roll in the eye, and make it keep right on rolling. They are proving that seasonal unemployment is no more necessary to successful business than seasonal divorce to successful marriage.

The American workman does not ask to be endowed with anybody's worldly goods. All he asks of his alliance with Industry is that it shall last long enough for him to build up his own endowment. He is willing to give to his job the best he has. In return, he wants a job that will give him all he is worth, for as long as he is worth it. He is tired of companionate jobs. He wants a job 'to have and to hold.'

'Red Day'

O N 'Red Day,' August 1, the Central Executive Committee of the Communist Party in the United States urged all loyal Communists to prepare for war. The Committee instructed them, in particular, to select one member in each shop or factory as a promising subject for military training, to serve as an officer 'when the time comes to arm the workers.'

Meanwhile, the Communists are trying to overthrow the Federal Government and set up a 'Workers' Government.' Toward this end, as directed by the Communist International in Russia, the loyal 'Reds' in this country are trying to organize 'shop nuclei' in every industry from coast to coast. Their slogan is 'Stir up Trouble: Organize the Unorganized: Get the Workers.' The orders from Russia especially stress the importance of spreading propaganda 'wherever jobs are scarce.'

This is nothing to worry about; but it is something we ought to know about. We can find out what we ought to know by reading an authoritative book by Charles G. Wood, Commissioner of Conciliation, Department of Labor, Washington, D.C. The title of the book, 'Reds and Lost Wages,' is well-chosen; for there are no 'Reds' where there are no lost wages.

The man who has a steady job, with steadily increasing real income, turns a deaf ear to the communist agitator. That is why, in recent years, the poor agitator in the United States has had a hard time agitating anybody but himself.

The 'Reds' have made *little* progress, for the reason that wages have made *much* progress.

As a matter of fact, there is one argument, and only one, which leaves the 'Red' agitator impotent and innocuous. That argument is a steady job.

'A Merry Heart Doeth Good'

A MERRY heart,' said Solomon, 'doeth good like a medicine.' And what is more conducive to a merry heart
than the exhilarating consciousness of 'getting ahead'? Compared with a wage of seven dollars a day, the conventional re-
cipe for keeping the doctor away is applesauce.

Dr. Prosperity, at last, is getting some deserved recognition
for his contributions to public health. The Medical Information Bureau assures us that 'good times' in business was one
of the reasons why New York hospitals in 1928 were no more
than 70 per cent occupied.

The average family income has increased in buying power
over 34 per cent since 1900. During the same period, the death
rate has dropped from 17.6 to 11.8 per thousand. In 1900, there
was an average loss of thirteen days per worker from illness.
By 1920, the loss had been reduced to seven days per worker.

At the same time, many hearts have been made merrier by
gains in per capita savings. We have only twice as many persons in this country as we had fifty years ago; but we have
twenty-five times as many dollars in bank deposits, and fifty
times as many in life insurance. Whatever relation there may
be between savings and health, one thing is certain: Freedom
from worry — even comparative freedom — is a powerful
tonic. Many men are suffering from high blood pressure. Many
more men are suffering from high economic pressure.

Some day, perhaps, the relation between health and wealth
will be so well known that the family physician will adopt a new
style of advice. Instead of repeating the glib formula, 'What
you require is rest,' he will say, 'My dear sir, what you need is
a steady job, with only voluntary rests.'

Industry itself will never have a merry heart until it is prepared to fill that prescription.

Therapeutic Value of Cash

DR. FOSTER KENNEDY told the New York Academy of Medicine recently that certain illnesses can best be cured by payment of damage money. We go further than that. We feel sure that the payment of money — damage money or any other kind — has a curative effect on most diseases.

Some diseases respond quickly to this treatment — malnutrition, for instance. We know a man who went for days without being able to digest anything at all, and then was instantly cured by the prospect of a pay envelope. This treatment is also indicated in ailments resulting from over-crowding, over-exposure, and high rent-pressure.

In fact, so great is the therapeutic value of cash that we wonder Dr. Kennedy's confrères don't save time by prescribing it outright, instead of using such polite circumlocutions as 'freedom from worry and drives in a car.' Why don't they say bluntly, 'What you need is substantial doses of money, taken at regular intervals?'

Perhaps they fear that some equally blunt patient will reply, 'That sounds good. Where'll I get the prescription filled?'

'Freedom from worry and drives in a car' may be a better prescription, after all. The patient can always find a place on a park bench where he can practice freedom from worry. And if he stays there long enough, some obliging policeman will fill the rest of the prescription.

Still, we venture to offer the medical profession a suggestion in line with current economic trends: Why not operate a chain of clinics in connection with a chain of employment agencies? A sort of interlocking doctorate. Then the good doctor could not only give the patient a good prescription, but — what is more to the point in many cases — tell him where to get it filled.

'Now It Toucheth Thee'

YOU say poverty some day will be abolished!' exclaimed the Doubter. 'Nonsense. You might as well say — er — '
For all we know, he is still struggling for a simile to express his scorn.

Twenty years ago, how easy it would have been! Think of what he could have said then: 'Yes, when I can fly to Europe!' Or — 'Sure it will, when I can turn a button and hear the King of England make a speech.' But what can a man fall back on these days? Perhaps the safest solution is to park scepticism in the attic, and not try to express it at all.

Poverty is doomed. Nobody ever wanted it for himself. Now nobody wants it even for the other fellow.

Employers once accepted, without question, the dictum that 'the great mass of wage-earners can never rise far above the lowest level of subsistence.' This, they supposed, was hard luck for 'the great mass of wage-earners.'

But gradually it dawned on them that low wages are hard luck for employers, as well. Lay off a wage-earner and a customer takes the count. Nothing but wages will revive him. So thoroughly has industry learned this lesson that, when a business recession developed after the collapse of the stock market in 1929, the Washington conferences of business leaders all began with one slogan: 'Wages must not be reduced.'

Wage-earners manifestly must rise several notches above 'the lowest level of subsistence' in order to be likely prospects for radios, automobiles, and silk stockings. Employers did a little intensive thinking about wages. The lowest-level-of-subsistence theory lost its glamour.

In the words of Job's friend: 'Now it toucheth thee, and thou art troubled.'

'Plenty of Cheap Labor'

ESTABLISH your business in this progressive city,' says a recent Chamber of Commerce advertisement. 'We offer free factory sites and plenty of cheap labor.'

England had plenty of cheap labor before the Revolution. For half a century, wages did not rise above three dollars a week. The workers were kept in poverty 'for their own good,' by deliberate intent of the upper classes.

Thomas Mun voiced the common belief of the time. 'Plenty and power,' he said, 'do make a nation vicious and improvident; so penury and want do make a people wise and industrious.'

'Hard times are a benefit,' declared Sir William Temple, 'because they encourage industry in the poor.'

'All manufacturers agree,' asserted the Reverend Joseph Townsend, 'that the poor are seldom diligent, except when labor is cheap and corn is dear.' And Josiah Tucker spoke for all the Lords and Landlords when he said: 'It is greatly for the public good if the price of labor is continually beat down.'

So they were kept poor. And therefore hopeless.

This led, naturally, to widespread drunkenness, a breakdown of sex morals, and enormous increases in sloth, obscenity, arson, robbery, and murder. It was in this 'pig-sty' era that the English working-classes reached the lowest depths of degeneracy.

But it was nothing to brag about!

Nearly everybody in the United States now knows that a city should be ashamed to advertise 'Plenty of Cheap Labor.'

Except, indeed, as a means of *abolishing* cheap labor by increasing the *demand* for labor!

'Nothing Down and Nothing a Week'

PLENTY of buyers and a business depression can no more go together than abundant rainfall and prolonged drought. Whenever the flow of money to consumers is sufficient, they do enough buying to sustain prosperity.

But is it any longer necessary to have money, when every merchant is begging us to buy goods for nothing down and nothing a week?

That raises the whole subject of instalment selling. 'It is the vilest system yet devised to create trouble, discontent, and unhappiness among the poor,' says George F. Johnson, President of the Endicott-Johnson Corporation.

'Far from it,' says A. R. Erskine, President of the Studebaker Corporation. 'Instalment selling is one of the greatest economic forward steps in modern times.'

It is not easy to say which of these two men is nearer the truth. The facts, however, are plain. Take automobiles, for example. Nobody doubts that this country produced over five million cars last year. Equally plain is the fact that cars were sold on time to the value of about three billion dollars. So people are now hunting around for places to park several million cars on which instalments of more than one billion dollars are still due.

To be sure, we have not yet been urged to buy chewing gum for a penny down and a penny a day. But millions of consumers are buying engagement rings on partial payments, and refrigerators, and oil heaters, and radio sets, and fur coats — not to mention false teeth. The Simple Simons of our day are not repulsed by unprogressive Piemen. 'Show me first your penny' is not the slogan of the 'Bigger, Better, and Busier Merchants.'

Is this a help or a hindrance? Is Mr. Erskine right, or is Mr. Johnson?

'Dignified Credit for All'

THE people of this country now have in their possession more than three billion dollars' worth of goods, bought on instalments, and not yet paid for. Is that a help or a hindrance to business?

This we know, anyway: All those goods actually were produced; somebody was paid wages for making them; somebody has them. Equally plain is the fact that a large part of those goods would not have been sold at all, had buyers been required to pay cash for them.

Even that is not the whole story. Had we not contrived to pass on to consumers three billion dollars' worth of goods in excess of what they have yet paid for, most of those goods would not have been produced. In that case, a large part of the salaries, wages, interest, and dividends, paid in connection with the production and sale of those goods, would not have been paid at all. It follows that the expansion of instalment selling during the past decade has increased employment, wealth, wages, and leisure.

How long can that go on? Forever, many people think.

But consider this fact: If consumers improve business in any one year by mortgaging their incomes one month in advance, they can sustain business at that level the next year only by mortgaging their income *two* months in advance; the next year, *three* months in advance; and so on. How far it is wise to carry this process, nobody knows; but any one can see that the possibilities are not unlimited.

Yet the stimulus to business of a given gain in instalment sales is not lasting. Larger and larger doses of the stimulant must be injected, merely to prevent a relapse. We need something more than devices for getting people deeper and deeper in debt. 'Dignified Credit for All' is not enough.

Puss-in-the-Corner Economics

THE Detroit City Council has announced its freedom from entangling mathematical alliances. It has passed a resolution proposing to 'relieve unemployment' by the simple device of firing the 1689 aliens on the city payroll and, presumably, hiring 1689 simon-pure Americans instead.

The resolution contains a qualifying clause. It provides that after the 1689 aliens have been alienated from their pay envelopes, 'department chiefs may make an investigation of each individual case with a view to re-employment, should there be extenuating circumstances.'

But can there be any 'extenuating circumstances' to the crime of being born in the wrong place? The 1689 aliens, to be sure, might plead that they were ignorant of the enormity of the crime at the time it was committed. But ignorance is no excuse.

It may be that these aliens, thrilled by the privilege of living in Detroit, have been doing an amount of work that will require twice as many native Americans. In that case, the Council's point is well taken. Unemployment will be relieved.

But if that is the point, why not put out a sign: 'Men Wanted. Only slow workers need apply.'

There is nothing to prevent any city, if the city fathers so elect, from firing a hundred blondes and hiring, instead, a hundred brunettes. But this little game of puss-in-the-corner will leave just as many job-seekers out in the cold.

Taking jobs away from aliens and bestowing them on Americans may be good politics, but it isn't good economics. It may relieve the patriotic fervor of its sponsors, but how can it 're-lieve unemployment'?

A man out of work is a man out of work, whether he was born in Ann Arbor or in Zanzibar.

Not Charity, but a Chance

THERE is a 'Good Will Industry' in Buffalo; another in Chicago; another in Cincinnati. The business of a Good Will Industry is salvaging waste materials and waste men. Cast-off things of all sorts are collected all over the city. Cast-off men of all sorts collect themselves at the Good Will portals. The waste men are put to work on the waste materials. The product is wealth — economic goods and human goodness.

Thus, the unemployed receive not alms but opportunity. And the community receives, in due course, its liabilities turned into assets.

Other lodging houses admit only those who have money. The Good Will houses admit only those who have no money.

The first night and the following morning, everything is free. 'Everything' includes a shower bath; a clean bed; a physician's diagnosis; treatment, if needed; a shave; a breakfast; and — what is sometimes more essential — a bath in rays of good will.

Then there is provided a real job. And presently, if the worker deserves it, he is promoted to learning a trade in the Good Will Industries on the Middlers' Floor. Later on, if his record is good enough, he is promoted to the Senior Floor, where he becomes a Big Brother to five newcomers. Eventually he is graduated, but not before he has been placed in a regular job.

Thus, while everybody has been talking about unemployment, the Good Will Industries have gone right ahead creating employment — giving men who would otherwise be idle, or marching in parades of protest, or driven to crime, a chance to earn a living by turning old rags into carpets.

Or any other old thing into something new and salable.

Thus derelicts have been started on the road to self-support and self-respect. They have received what they wanted: not charity, but a chance.

Chores *vs.* Charity

BEFORE the era of large-scale production, when the typical family lived on the farm, there were always chores to do. Nobody was ever out of a job. But in this era of mass production, many millions of men and women either find work with huge corporations, or find no work at all. At times, a distressing number find no work at all.

'Grant them doles,' says Senator Brookhart; and he has introduced a bill which calls for a Federal appropriation of fifty million dollars for the purpose.

But the unemployed do not want doles; they want jobs. That is always the demand on the banners in the out-of-work demonstrations of radical groups. And in that particular demand, the radicals always find sympathy.

Moreover, every nation which has tried doles has come to grief. Doles do not cure the disease of unemployment; they aggravate it. England, after struggling along for years under a system of doles, finds more applicants than ever. Doles destroy self-respect and the will to work. They make a bad situation worse. As a matter of fact, a resort to doles on the part of any government is a confession of failure to solve its chief economic problem.

Anyway, Senator Brookhart's fifty million dollar appropriation would not go far. At best, it would provide only one dollar a week for seventeen weeks, to three millions of the unemployed. That is not even a temporary solution of the problem. And at the end of seventeen weeks, there would be a demand for more doles.

For doles do not create jobs: they create loafers.

Since Senator Brookhart wants to help the jobless, we suggest that he arrange, *in advance of trouble*, for the speeding-up of government construction programs. Give the unemployed what they want, Senator — chores, not charity.

'Part-Time Mothers'

ONE way to find jobs for men is to take jobs away from women. 'Send them back to their homes, where they belong,' says an editorial. 'There are too many part-time mothers.'

The first objection to this cure for unemployment is that it is no cure at all. It only shifts the burden from one sex to the other. Must we be prepared to hear, next, that some city proposes to remedy a shortage in its water supply by running water from one of its reservoirs into another? We cannot too often remind ourselves that the only real cure for too few jobs is more jobs.

Another objection to taking jobs away from women, is that women, as everybody knows, are now doing, *outside* the home, a large part of the work which women used to do *in* the home. Consider the ever-increasing range of their activities in canneries, textile mills, clothing factories, laundries, bakeries, restaurants, hospitals, schools. Most of this work, or its crude counterpart, used to be done on the farm.

There is still plenty of truth in the old adage, 'Woman's place is in the home'; but there is just as much truth in the new adage: 'Woman's place is where her work is.'

And a large part of her work is where the industrial revolution has put it.

Doing that work, she is happier, as a rule, than otherwise she could possibly be. She is happier, as any one can see at a glance, than the woman who is running around from one so-called pleasure resort to another, looking for something to do. The wage-earner is happier because she is more serene, resourceful, self-reliant, purposeful. Usually, too, she is more alert mentally. She is a better citizen and a better companion.

And in many cases, it cannot be denied, she is a better mother — even though only a 'part-time mother.'

How Many Men are Unemployed?

HOW many men are without jobs? Nobody knows. Discussions about this question have the merry-go-round futility of the classic conversation between two men who had dined too well.

'D'yer know Bill Brown?' asked one.

'What's his name?' demanded the other.

'Who?' inquired the first.

With all the efforts we are making to solve the problem of unemployment, nobody knows exactly what the problem is.

Lack of information constantly hampered the 1921 Conference on Unemployment. It reported that little could be accomplished, because there was no statistical basis upon which to begin. 'Nor is this the first occasion,' the report concludes, 'when public conferences have been embarrassed by a lack of such necessary facts.'

Nor was it the last occasion. For in January of 1928, when so many men lost their jobs that the United States Senate was stirred to days of discussion, no dependable statistics were available. The Department of Labor declared that it had 'no information whatever concerning the numbers unemployed at this time or any other time.' Later on, it is true, the Secretary of Labor made a long report to the Senate, which was widely interpreted to mean that only 1,874,050 were unemployed. Actually, the Secretary gave no statistics whatever concerning the unemployed. Estimates ran all the way from two million to seven million. Some Democrats said the number was appalling; some Republicans said they didn't think so.

All of which was repeated in the winter of 1929–30.

Yet with the aid of a national system of employment exchanges, we can obtain the necessary information at a trifling cost. Trifling, at least, compared with the billions that are lost in every big business slump!

Bigger, Better, and Busier Statistics

THE tiniest thing ever measured in the universe is an electron which is less than a millionth of a millionth of an inch in width. The hugest thing yet measured is a star system which is more than a thousand million trillion miles across. These measurements have been reported by the Director of the Harvard Astronomical Observatory. Such facts, he adds, give 'a modest view of man's place in the universe.'

To try to conceive of such a universe is one way to stimulate the imagination. Another way is to try to conceive what might happen if, right here on this dot of the universe known as the United States of America, we measured economic phenomena with equal scope and accuracy.

If we did, we should always know the exact size of the national income and how many men and women were unemployed. Instead, we measure the national income only roughly, and too late to be of any use in an emergency. And we have never, except in the Census of 1930, come within a million of knowing the numbers of the unemployed. As a result, public policy has been determined by hunches instead of facts, guesses instead of measurements.

Yet it is just as easy to count men as to count stars; just as easy to measure the extent of unemployment as to measure the extent of the solar system. And the most insignificant of our jobless fathers looms larger before his hungry children than the hugest of our stars. One can say that, while still keeping 'a modest view of man's place in the universe.'

'God's in His Heaven,' and He has not deputized us to run it. The chore He *has* given us is to see that 'all's well with the world' — our own world of work and wages.

To do that chore, we need — first, last, and in between times — Bigger, Better, and Busier Statistics.

Why Pick on Oregon?

DO you know the fate of the -RA verb-form in the Golden Age of Spain? The chances are that you do not. Until recently, the rest of the world remained in ignorance of this tragedy. Now we learn that 'the -RA verb-form lost its indicative value about the year 1450'; and then, incredible as it seems, 'virtually ceased so to function for almost four centuries.' A professor in the State University of Oregon has just found this out by counting all the verbs in 580,000 lines of Spanish prose and poetry.

Now if some other professor will kindly compute the ratio between the sufferings of a Spanish verb, laid off for four centuries, and those of an American wage-earner, laid off for four weeks, we shall know about where we stand. Not exactly, for we do not know how many workers in the State of Oregon ceased to function in the present year of Our Lord. Yet the fate of jobless fathers is as tragic as the fate of parts of speech. And modern American human beings are just as interesting, and just as easy to count, as medieval Spanish verb-forms.

But why pick on Oregon? As yet, no other State has collected enough information to tackle the problem intelligently.

We need facts about the unemployed in every State. Who are they? How many are recent immigrants? What is the immediate cause of their troubles? How long have they been out of work? What is their skill and experience? How many are dependent on them? What other sources of income have they? What are the local difficulties and prospects?

Also — a very important matter — we need such information concerning those who are counted as employed, but who have only part-time jobs. And we need to know how many young men and women are seeking jobs for the first time. They are part of the problem. Without answers to such questions, and many more, we cannot deal with the problem intelligently.

First Find the Jobless

WE talk a great deal about solving the problem of unemployment without making any effort to find out
exactly what the problem is. Take your own city, for example.
Has any one found out what per cent of your wage-earners are
unemployed? Does any one know what per cent are idle because they can't find work, and what per cent are idle because
they won't work?

Has anybody taken the trouble to find out exactly who they
are, or why they are what they are? Does anybody know how
many families they represent, or how long each worker has
been without a job? Does anybody know for what proportion
of these men each industry is responsible?

Philadelphia can answer these questions about its unemployed, and a hundred other questions; for here is a city —
praise be — that has gone directly about the business of finding
out. Instead of getting red in the face *arguing* about the number of unemployed, the people of Philadelphia have taken the
extraordinary course of *counting* them.

This, in part, is what Philadelphia learned on a certain day in
March, 1929:

10.4 per cent of the wage-earners were unemployed
15.6 per cent of the families had unemployed members
75. per cent were idle because they could find no work
4.3 per cent were idle because they refused to work
11.5 per cent in industrial sections were out of work
1.8 per cent of workers in professions were out of work
30. per cent of workers were idle in certain blocks
12.5 per cent of the idle were in building trades
50.6 per cent had been idle more than three months

Certainly, this approach to the problem offers more hope to
the sufferers than the usual approach through inherited prejudice.

What the Go-Getter is Getting

ONCE upon a time, the only difference between a go-getter and a steam riveter seemed to be the fact that the go-getter produced his effects without mechanical aid. At that time, we used to wonder where the go-getter was going, and what he was going to get when he got there.

Now we know. The up-to-date go-getter is going to the bottom of business conditions; and when he gets there, he is going to get facts. The old go-getter's activities were largely vocal. The new go-getter's theme is: 'Face the facts. If there aren't any facts to face, go-get some. Build business as engineers build bridges. Take measurements before taking measures.'

Chain stores, for instance, learned by this method that whenever fifteen persons pass a certain corner, one comes in to buy. The directors wasted no time in argument. They hired a man with a clicking machine to stand in front of the location under consideration and count the traffic. By thus getting the facts, they developed a science of locations.

'If you subtract 14 from 92,' asked a teacher, 'what's the difference?'

'Yeah,' said Johnny sympathetically, 'I think it's a lotta boloney, too.'

The first Federal census of unemployment came, at last, in 1930. But to the old go-getter type of politician, the determination by actual count of the difference between the number of real-unemployed and the number of guessed-unemployed is a 'lotta boloney.' In the face of facts, he cannot hammer away any longer, like a steam riveter, on assertions that are shot full of holes by the facts. But to business men, Mr. Hoover's passion for collecting facts is a cheery indication that our Biggest Business is substituting science for supposition; counting for conjecturing. It is getting facts to face and facing them.

We Prosper by Planning to Prosper

NO nation can prosper to-day except by getting ready to prosper to-morrow.

One way to get ready is by building public works — highways, harbors, bridges, and the like. The construction of public works provides jobs, and thus enables men to take goods off the markets. Not that governments can increase consumers' funds merely by taking money away from them as taxes and giving it back to them as wages. But when State and local governments collect only five billions in taxes and spend about seven billions, a large amount of money which is spent on highways, public buildings, and the rest, comes not from taxes, but from loans.

Now many of these loans, directly or indirectly, involve an expansion of bank credit, which means new money in circulation. Such loans, therefore, help dealers to clear their shelves, and unemployed men to find jobs.

In effect, public works are bought on instalments; and so, as long as the volume increases, business is stimulated, as by the growth of any other kind of instalment buying. Thus, partly through the right rate of growth of public works, the right flow of money to consumers actually has come at times. But it has come only by chance. And chance, sooner or later, brings too large a flow of money or too small a flow; too much money spent by governments, as in 1919; or too little, as in 1921 and 1930. In either case the result is business depression.

For corrective influences do not automatically get to work, except far too slowly and at tragic costs in human suffering. There is a vicious spiral of inflation, and an even more vicious spiral of deflation; and there always will be, as long as we rely on chance.

Such gambling is not necessary. We can have prosperity by planning prosperity.

Prosperous Because We Ride

HOW great is our debt to the builders of the automobile industry! Theirs has been the vision, theirs the energy, theirs the faith, that has moved mountains of discouragement. Always, according to dire predictions, the automobile business has been about to collapse. Always, the saturation point has been nearly reached.

Nothing daunted, the builders have gone blithely on. With eagerness to seize new ideas, with quick response to new desires, with amazing technical skill, and with rapid reduction of costs, they have trebled the output of their workers per man-hour. Thus they have given us a highly complicated and efficient piece of machinery at a lower cost per pound than a tub of butter.

And thus they have created an industry which employs three million workers; an industry which yields 700 million dollars in taxes; an industry — non-existent thirty years ago — which now stands first in the value of its products; an industry which is largely responsible for the epoch-making extension of public highways and for suburban development; an industry which has put new life into the whole world of industry, and made a hundred million people more prosperous than otherwise they could have been.

We have said nothing here about the effect of the automobile on health and recreation, or its influence in sending congested populations into the suburbs, and in making rural life more livable. It is our opinion that the automobile has made a large net addition, not only to the passing pleasures, but as well to the durable satisfactions of life. Concerning the effects of the industry on material welfare, however, nobody's mere opinion matters.

We do not ride in automobiles because we are prosperous. We are prosperous because we ride in automobiles.

The Circulating Medium

MORE jobs and bigger payrolls require more money in circulation — meaning by more 'money,' more currency and more bank credit.

A given volume of money in circulation makes possible a given volume of business, on a given price-level. More business requires more money. More money means more wages and more employment.

That is because enough money in circulation means enough buying of commodities to keep pace with increased production; and enough buying means an end to falling commodity prices. That encourages business to employ more men and carry larger payrolls.

On the other hand, nothing is so discouraging to business as a prolonged period of falling prices. To many manufacturers, that means a loss in the raw materials which they *must* buy — a loss so great as to wipe out profits. Such manufacturers discharge all or part of their workers.

The Federal Reserve System induces business men to put more money into circulation in three ways:

By reducing interest rates.

By buying securities in the open market.

By issuing encouraging statements regarding money and banking conditions.

But there is little the System can do, directly, to employ more workers and enlarge payrolls. Business men must do that. The way to do it is by confidently going ahead, using the available funds for enlarging factories, improving equipment, extending railroads, starting new industries — in short, making to-day prosperous by preparing for a more prosperous to-morrow.

The way *not* to do it is for business men to stand, with reluctant feet, where their own responsibilities and those of the Federal Reserve meet.

The Blessing of Fire and Flood

NOT long ago, the Green Mountain State had an unusually prosperous year. The unemployed were put to work. Trade received a new impetus. Standards of living were raised. All this happened because the most destructive flood in the history of Vermont created jobs, increased payrolls, boosted sales, and fired business men with new confidence. So great was the enthusiasm of those that did business after the great waters, that only good taste restrained luncheon clubs from singing gratefully (tune of 'Smiles') 'The Flood That Filled Our State With Wages.'

The stimulus of the great flood will pass, and jobs will be harder to find. It will be the story, told again, of San Francisco after the great fire. But surely the people of Vermont — the shrewd and practical stock from which Calvin Coolidge sprang — need not stand helplessly by until Providence blesses the State with another calamity.

The World War was also a powerful stimulus to business. Factories ran full blast. There were plenty of jobs. Production of wealth reached new heights. Even the farmers ceased to complain of their lot. The reason was not patriotism: the greatest gains came *before* the United States entered the War. The cause of this sudden spurt of business was the sudden creation of an adequate market. Demand increased by leaps and bounds. For the first time in a generation, there were buyers at hand for more than the country could produce.

Must we go to war again in order to create markets?

Must we pray, 'Give us this day a flood,' in order that tomorrow we may earn our daily bread?

Must we lose lives by fire, in order to save lives by jobs?

Surely we can manage to prosper without recourse to the blessing of fire, flood, and battle.

'The Economics of Original Sin'

MANY men look upon business depression as a disease which must run its course. Such men hold that nothing can be done to prevent slumps, or to speed recovery. Addicts of this doctrine, says *The Business Week*, hold that business depressions are inevitable and salutary. They look upon such afflictions much as certain sects in the Far East look upon the eye diseases of children. All such calamities come from on high. Any attempt of man to interfere with divine law is perilous and immoral.

This is the view taken by those Doctors of Despair — now at large in this country — whom *The Business Week* calls Statistical Sadists. These queer fellows gloat over sad statistics. They chant their eternal song, 'Wait and See.' They worship 'the twin saints Action and Reaction — the Amos and Andy of Economic Law.' And their favorite exercise is The Long Run.

If any one suggests to these Doctors of Despair that the run might be shortened — that increased capital expenditures, public and private, under the aggressive leadership of the Federal Government, might create jobs and cut short the sentence of suffering — they throw up their hands in horror. 'They point to the tables of the Economic Law and the moral lessons to be drawn from the investigations of Adam (Smith) in the Economic Eden of eighteenth century England.'

A business depression, in their view, is the punishment for original sin. To try to escape the prolonged process of penance, is to try to cheat the gods. It is an attempt to defy natural laws by a kind of bootstrap levitation.

After listening to such preaching, it was cheering to every one except the Statistical Sadists to hear President Hoover say to the United States Chamber of Commerce: 'I do not accept that fatalistic view.'

'Specific Gravity'

THE Road to Plenty is not necessarily a roller-coaster. Every business depression valley can be exalted — and kept exalted. Every business boom mountain can be made low — and kept low.

But not by playing oratorical hop-scotch in the cow-path to nowhere. Ironing out business is like any other ironing: it requires a minimum of conversation and a maximum of technique.

We should be amazed if an engineer, when asked to submit plans for constructing a subway, responded with a lofty oration on the sacredness of human life. We know that human life is sacred. We assume that he knows it. What we want to examine is his specifications.

In a speech before the Chamber of Commerce of the United States, Mr. Hoover recently made specific recommendations. They were about the new Road to Plenty which we are all eager to travel. With an engineer's precision, he has carefully surveyed the Old Road — the one that was always being washed out by heavy rains. He does not think that we should scrap the Old Road and construct an entirely new one. He favors using the original road-bed; but he urges us to fill in the gullies and level off the bumps. He plans to appoint a group of expert Road Commissioners to tell us how to get our Road in shape and keep it in shape.

In this speech, Mr. Hoover said little about the 'sacredness of human life.' He did not move his audience to tears. But his recommendations for making human beings happier and more secure in their happiness were to the point.

His speech was more conspicuous for gravity than for pathos. But the gravity was specific gravity. And, after all, it is the specifications that count!

Long-Range Planning to Plan

OVER and over again, economists, business men, and statesmen have recommended that the construction of public works be postponed in periods of rapid business expansion, and pushed forward in periods of contraction. That policy was advocated in 1923 by the President's Conference on Unemployment. The American Federation of Labor indorsed the policy; also numerous chambers of commerce. Mr. Coolidge expressed his approval, as well as Mr. Mellon and Mr. Hoover. Not to be outdone by Republicans, the Democrats put a plank in their platform calling for long-range planning of public works.

A remarkable unanimity of opinion. And what have been the results? Up to 1929, virtually no results at all.

The reasons are plain. Without the guidance of timely data on unemployment, wages, retail buying, and the like, there is no means of knowing just what to do, or just when to do it.

Moreover, nobody is now responsible for carrying out the policy, and nobody has the power. This is one of the many cases in which everybody agrees that it would be splendid for somebody to do something, but nobody does it.

The situation is this: No Federal department has any money to spend which has been appropriated with a view to stabilizing business; no department has sufficient leeway in the use of its funds to accomplish much, even if it wanted to do so; and no department has sufficient information as a basis for action.

As long as that situation prevails, everybody might talk himself hoarse in favor of allocating public expenditures with reference to the needs of business, without having the slightest effect on business.

Since the proposal is constructive, it is time we found it a pair of overalls and a boss and put it to work constructing. Long-Range Planning to Plan will never get us anywhere.

Can We Conquer Unemployment?

AT the Conference of Governors in New Orleans, in the fall of 1928, Mr. Hoover requested the coöperation of all the States with the Federal Government in using public expenditures for the purpose of sustaining business and preventing unemployment. He asked preparation for emergency action a year in advance of the stock market emergency of 1929. He advocated increased employment of men on public works, in proportion to decreased employment on private enterprises.

How can such a plan be made effective?

First of all, there must be planning of public works. Decisions concerning projects to be started in time of special need must be reached well in advance of a decline of business. Also, as far as feasible, blue prints, specifications, and contracts must be ready. Other advance arrangements must be made so that public credit can be used promptly when the need arises.

In order to determine when the need does arise, we must have better measurements of economic trends. Most important of these for the purpose are index numbers of unemployment, wages, and retail prices. An index number enables us to sum up miles of statistics in a single figure. By means of two such figures, we can compare millions of prices paid at one time with millions of prices paid at another time.

These three requisites — construction plans, public credit, and economic indexes — will enable Federal, State, and local governments not only to increase expenditures promptly when private business lags, but also to decrease expenditures promptly when private business forges ahead too rapidly. Thus governments may help to sustain trade and employment.

We can conquer unemployment as we conquer fire — with emergency apparatus which is ready to emerge at the first alarm.

More Jobs in Time of Need

GOVERNMENTS — Federal, State, and local — should spend less money on public works when prices rise and business begins to boom; more money when business depression sets in. This is part of a sound policy for preventing unemployment.

More money for what? For whatever is most needed, as determined in the usual way. Projects are already planned for national highways, inland waterways, parks, buildings, harbors, reforestation, and reclamation of waste lands. Construction on these projects can be pushed forward or held back, as the general business situation requires. Nothing but the expense holds them back now. Nothing else kept us from taking adequate flood prevention measures in the Mississippi Valley long ago.

Such projects can be so financed as to increase wages throughout the country. Thus we can sustain business and at the same time acquire wealth. Public works built in that way might actually cost the country nothing; for if they were not built, the country might lose more than they cost, through the idleness of men and capital.

Contracts for public works should be let when private enterprise needs their stimulus. Timing, not time, is the essence of these contracts.

Imagine what would happen if the Federal Government — the largest consumer, the largest spender, in the world — announced its intention of carrying out this plan as far as feasible. Most business men would expect that business would be good; little danger of inflation or deflation; just an orderly market, keeping up with production.

And because of the widespread conviction that business would be good, nearly every private business concern would so act as to help to *make* business good.

Prosperity Plans

SOME people doubt the feasibility of sustaining employment through the expansion of public and private construction. How, they ask, can a horde of idle Pennsylvania coal-miners or Maine shoemakers suddenly be moved to Colorado to build a dam?

The answer is that no such migration of labor is necessary. The plan calls for increased expenditures in *every* State, in order to provide additional jobs, when, as, and if needed.

Even so, how can such construction as buildings, railways, merchant marine, public utilities, and public works provide jobs for all those who want jobs? When a business depression sets in, most of the men and women who lose their jobs cannot put up steel structures, or pour cement, or even dig ditches.

That is true. But it is also true that expansion of construction adds to the demand for cement, steel, glass, lumber, and hundreds of other commodities — trucks, tools, architects' plans, and all the rest. For that reason, not all the money that is spent on a local job goes into local pay envelopes. It is impossible, for example, to spend 165 million dollars on the Boulder Dam, or even to spend ten million dollars on the proposed East Boston tunnel — if this is a net addition to the wages of the country — without increasing the demand for labor throughout the country.

Moreover, nearly all the wages paid out, directly or indirectly, in building such a tunnel — or in building anything else — are promptly spent for shoes, candy, theater tickets, gasoline, ice, and the countless other things which make up family budgets. This increases the demand for labor in every industry.

The plan is sound. The expansion of private capital facilities and public works, at the right rate, is all that is needed, ordinarily, to keep men employed and business active.

Is the 'Pretty Theory' Practical?

IS it possible to speed up enough public construction at certain times, and to postpone enough at other times to prevent unemployment?

Such a plan, we are told, 'makes a pretty theory, but it is not practicable.' When the Government needs a new post-office at Boston, it needs a new post-office at Boston. It cannot put off construction merely because business happens to be headed for a boom. When California needs a new highway, it needs a new highway, no matter what the index numbers of employment show. Likewise, the Mississippi Valley needs flood prevention; needs it now. Floods are impulsive, self-willed young things. When one of them gets the urge for self-expression, it isn't in nature for it to stall around waiting for advice from statisticians.

There is something to this objection, but not much. Actually, the amount of money that is spent in any given year on post-offices and highways and flood prevention is not determined mainly by the degree of need. If a thousand miles of roads are built this year in New York State, it is not because those roads are particularly needed *this* year. They were needed last year.

And why only a thousand miles? Almost as urgent a need could be shown for two thousand miles.

Not merely need, but a hundred other considerations now determine the outlay each year by Federal, State, and local governments. Surely, it is wise to give weight to one more consideration. It is wise to take into account the effect of such expenditures on wages and employment.

It is a 'pretty' theory; but it is also, we submit, intensely 'practical.' Any one who supposes that these two terms are mutually exclusive should take an hour off and re-read 'Gentlemen Prefer Blondes.'

The Largest Spender in the World

THE Federal Government is the largest business in the world; the largest consumer; the largest spender. As such, it inevitably affects prices, markets, and public confidence. So the question is not whether the Government through its expenditures shall influence trade and employment, but how it shall exert its influence most intelligently.

Government expenditures are at all times additions to private expenditures. There are times when private expenditures are too large; other times when they are too small. The Government can regulate part of its own expenditures accordingly. Thus it can help to maintain the balance of supply and demand in the markets, without exercising any control whatever over private spending.

Recently, for example, the Government has been considering tax reductions, increased wages of Federal employees, tariff revisions, expenditures for flood control, reclamation of waste lands, changes in money rates, and payments of the public debt. All such measures affect business. Under certain conditions, such measures help business. Under other conditions, they just as surely hurt business.

But the Government now spends its four billion dollars a year with scarcely any consideration of the effect of these expenditures upon trade and employment. Even when it becomes clear that business is indulging in a boom, the Government does not slacken its competition with private concerns for labor and materials. So, also, when a business depression sets in, the Government goes ahead, without greatly enlarging its prearranged program.

The least we can say is that the largest spender in the world, in spending its four billions a year, should take business conditions into account.

Storm Signals for Business

HOW can we expect business men to favor further Government control of business?

We expect no such thing. All we propose is that the Government, directly and indirectly, shall employ more men when jobs are scarce, and fewer men when jobs are plentiful.

This proposal gives the Government no new powers; it merely calls for the more intelligent use of its present powers. The Government now has sole power to levy Federal taxes, expend money for public works, regulate the currency, impose duties, fix wages of its employees, borrow money for Federal uses, and pay its debts.

In exercising these powers, the Government now acts one way or the other, with or without adequate guidance, with or without due consideration of the trend of prices, employment, and money in circulation. Thus the Government affects business. Inevitably. Even those who cry 'less Government in business' do not propose to destroy these powers.

As a matter of fact, the policy which we propose means *less* interference with business; for it provides better business information, more promptly and more widely distributed.

Under this policy, morerover, the Government makes its own expenditures with reference to business needs, slackening its competition with private concerns for men and materials when competition is keenest, and adding to the income of buyers when buying is falling off. That also means *less* Government interference with business.

The Government now puts up storm signals at every port without boarding the ships and telling the captains what to do. Surely the Government could announce that it is, or is not, a favorable time for expansion of plant without taking control of the Steel Corporation.

Government Interference With Business

IN 1929, for the first time in our history, a President of the United States took aggressive leadership in guiding private business through a crisis. Yet all over the country, strange to say, we heard nothing but praise for this action. What has become of all those who used to cry out against Government interference with business?

The fact is, we have all seen a new light. We understand now, as never before, that the business of these United States — including the business of the Federal Government, which is the largest business of the world — is so gigantic that no private agency is able to guide its destiny.

Collective leadership is indispensable. Such leadership can be furnished at times by private organizations; but there are sure to be times when private leadership is not enough. That is necessarily so, because each business man must first look out for his own interests. In a situation like that following a crash of the stock market, few individuals dare to act alone. Few are even able to act alone. In such a situation, relying on individual initiative is relying on chaos.

In the past, when a depression threatened, it seemed wise for each business concern to curtail orders, reduce payrolls, postpone expansion of plant, pay off bank loans — in short, do precisely what would help to bring on the depression. This was good policy for the individual concern, provided concerted action would not be taken on a large enough scale to forestall the depression.

But the prearranged and coördinated action of private and public business, under sufficiently prompt, liberal, and aggressive Federal leadership, would make it in the interests of each individual to do precisely what is good for business as a whole.

Let us have more of such 'interference with business.'

Black and White

FOR more than a century, the speeding up of public works in time of business depression was urged as one means of keeping men employed and trade active. Yet for more than a century, results were next to nothing at all.

The trouble seemed to be the one mentioned by Mark Twain in connection with the weather. Everybody talked about it; but nobody did anything about it.

As a matter of fact, most of those in authority seemed to think that nothing *could* be done about it. They insisted that business depressions, like tornadoes, were the result of natural law. And what can you do to stop a tornado?

In the business slump of 1920–21, these *Do-Nothing Politicians* were in control. The contracts which they awarded for public works and public utilities, far from showing the needed gains, actually fell off. Moreover, they kept on falling off throughout the period of business revival.

During the business cycle, 1924–27, however, the *Do-Nothing Politicians* lost control. For the first time in our history, largely increased expenditures on public works preceded the revival of business in general.

Again, in the slump of 1929–30, construction of public works and utilities was speeded up for the avowed purpose of curbing the decline of business and hastening the recovery.

The carrying out of this policy was too long delayed, and it was crude and confined. *Nevertheless, something actually was done.* Thus, the planning and timing of public works with reference to the ups and downs of business has become, at last, an accepted national policy. That is a real achievement. There is all the difference in the world between doing something and doing nothing. There is no greater difference between black and white.

'The National Fascist Council'

THE action of the Government in mobilizing the Nation's forces, in the fall of 1929, brought about a general agreement to maintain wage-rates and proceed with construction programs. Possibly it saved a million workers from losing their jobs during the winter months. Yet the Communists condemned this act as a 'gigantic bloc of capitalism against the workers.'

'The Communist Party,' we read, 'accepts the challenge of Hoover's National Fascist Council. American workers will not be willing victims of this new cut-throat drive of the capitalists! In this dirty work of crushing the workers' resistance —'

But before we get lost in this flight of rhetoric, let us descend to earth and get a view of the facts. To precisely what extent have American workers been victims of the capitalists?

To this extent: The average hourly money earnings of some 14 million workers are 125 per cent above the average for 1914. The length of the standard working week has been reduced 15 per cent. Annual real earnings in manufacturing establishments have risen 34 per cent. The result is that workers as a whole, with fewer hours of work, can now buy with their wages at least 30 per cent more than they could buy fifteen years ago. They have the highest standard of living ever enjoyed by any people, anywhere in the world.

This has resulted almost entirely from increased productivity, which in turn has resulted largely from new inventions, elimination of waste, mass production, better management, and the Federal Reserve System.

All this came about, not through the constructive efforts of Communists, but in spite of their destructive efforts. It was largely the achievement of leaders of American industry, notable among them being the men contemptuously referred to by the Communist Party as 'Hoover's National Fascist Council.'

Was the Hoover Policy Sound?

FOLLOWING the stock market debacle of 1929, President Hoover assumed leadership of the nation's business with the avowed purpose of increasing capital expenditures, public and private, thereby sustaining trade and employment. Recalling his appeal to the governors at New Orleans in 1928, the President again asked the States and cities to coöperate with the Federal Government in expanding public works. At the same time, he urged private business to do its part.

Eight months later, the country floundered in the trough of a major business depression. Volume of trade was far below normal. Volume of unemployment was far above normal. Stock prices again struck panic levels. Pessimism prevailed.

Does this prove that the President's policy was unsound? It certainly does not, for the Federal Government scarcely tried the policy. In the first six months of 1930, the Treasury Department awarded contracts for new Government construction amounting to a paltry $32,480,000. At best, this amount could not supply one cent out of every dollar in wages lost during the same period. All this time the Wagner bill, which called for the expenditure of an additional $150,000,000 on public works, was ignored or scoffed at by the Federal Administration. To be sure, the amount should have been ten times as large; but $150,000,000 was better than nothing. In point of fact, the total amount of money which actually went into pay envelopes in the first half of 1930, as the result of Federal emergency measures, was not enough to restore one per cent of the lost volume of trade.

The answer of private business to the call of the President was prompt and substantial. The answer of public business was neither.

The policy urged by President Hoover was sound; but it was not half tried.

Guidance in Time of Inflation

FROM the pioneering leadership of the Federal Government, after the stock market collapse of 1929, we now know something about the actual working of such a plan in a period of deflation. But how would this plan operate in a period of industrial expansion and price inflation? What, for example, would a Federal Budget Board, entrusted with the administration of the plan, have done in the inflation years of 1917–20?

We ought to point out, first of all, that such a situation could not have developed under the plan as proposed, for restraining influences would have been brought to bear long before prices went as high as they did in those skyrocketing years.

Certain things, however, the Board would have done at that time. It would have called public attention to the dangers. It would have published unidentified statistics to show which branches of business were riding fastest to a fall. Still further to curb the rise in prices, the Board would have opposed reduction in taxes and the unnecessary payment of public debts and all avoidable increases of the money in circulation. At the same time, the Board would have authorized no further expenditures of the public funds subject to its own control.

Moreover, the Board would have explained why public business, as far as practicable, should cease competing with private business for workers and materials. The Board would have had the intelligent coöperation of a large number of States and cities. This is evident from the aid which was given in 1929–30 in answer to the President's call. The Board would then have watched every aspect of the situation, in order to measure the effects of its acts and to prevent a sharp reaction.

Thus, even in the post-war boom, the Board could have done much to bring about a slow and orderly movement of prices.

Why Wait for a Hurricane?

IN the spring of 1922, Massachusetts was swept by a hurricane, and great damage was done to highways. The Governor asked for a special reparation fund and got it. An order was given to place two hundred unemployed veterans on the job. Three thousand five hundred men applied. So great was the crush that the Governor, to reach his office, had to force his way through the crowded corridors.

In nearly all cases, the men assigned to the jobs were married veterans, with children, or with dependent mothers and fathers. Were these men really anxious to work?

This is what the Department Commander says:

'On the day the work was to start, there was a terrific rain and hailstorm. The place was about eleven miles from the center of Boston. Still, many of these men who lacked the necessary ten cents for car fare walked the whole distance. Some of the hikers had to leave their homes before six o'clock to be at work on time. It was discovered that many of the men reached the scene of the work with their feet out through their shoes; and several men were without underwear. They carried on through the storm, and worked all day without gloves. Although many of the men were drenched to the skin, on the third day only eight were absent. Police officers were designated to carry the pay to the homes of those who did not report. The officers found that every man who had not reported was sick in bed, and in practically every case was living in destitute circumstances.'

There are *always* some men in need of jobs. There are *always* some public works that ought to be started. We can *always* plan accordingly — quietly, economically — getting blue prints ready and specifications and public credit. We do not have to wait for a hurricane.

A Niagara Built to Order

WHEN the Boulder Dam is completed, the waters of the Colorado River will generate as much power as is now developed at Niagara Falls. The reservoir above the dam, one hundred miles long, will hold enough water to cover the State of Kentucky to a depth of one foot. Uncontrolled, as at present, the Colorado River is turbulent and destructive a part of the year, and all but dried up the rest of the year. Controlled, the Colorado River will irrigate 100,000 now barren acres; develop the rich mines of Nevada; light one hundred cities and run their factories; make possible the feeding, housing, and clothing of ten million more people than now live in the Southwest. In short, the Colorado River will become an asset instead of a liability. All these facts are vouched for by Elwood Mead, Commissioner of the United States Bureau of Reclamation.

The Boulder Dam is a stupendous undertaking, soundly conceived, and approved by several engineers of international reputation. But it will cost a lot of money!

Yes, the dam, power plant, and All-American Canal will cost about $165,000,000. The aqueduct, which is to carry the water to the coast counties of California, will cost another $165,000,000 — probably more. That certainly is a lot of money. Directly and indirectly, it will provide jobs for sixteen thousand men for eight years. Three hundred freight cars a day will be required to carry the materials, all of which will provide jobs for somebody.

Labor-saving inventions are now throwing more than sixteen thousand men out of work every month. Their chief hope of new jobs lies in new projects. Undoubtedly, the Boulder Dam will keep at work many men who would otherwise be idle. In so far as the Boulder Dam does that, this large project will cost the country nothing at all.

Hardening of the Arteries

O. HENRY, agreeing that the circulating medium should circulate, offered himself as a 'full-growed artery therefor.' Wisconsin, perceiving that money follows trade, and that trade flows along highways, invitingly labels each of its principal roads 'Main Artery.' And now, having provided channels for the circulating medium, why not make it flow through them more evenly?

Here is one way: Select a time when money is sluggish; when it is seen less and less frequently on the street, and appears to be about to crawl in somewhere for a long nap.

Call in the Road Commissioner and tell him graciously that the Legislature has decided to make an appropriation for some of that road paving he has been hounding it about.

After convincing the Commissioner that you mean business, get him to select some of his pet paving projects — well-traveled roads between salient points. Main arteries. Have him hire a crew of men not otherwise engaged (there'll be plenty of them, as soon as money begins to yawn) and supply them with some nice big consignments of cement. Good intentions are said to be used for the purpose elsewhere, but cement is more durable.

Then, when the hardening of your arteries is well under way, stand back, and watch the circulating medium circulate.

It will do your heart good. Also your cash register.

First, it will circulate into workmen's pockets. From there, as a point of departure (and quick departure) it will set out on a sort of Chamber of Commerce 'pepping-up' tour, visiting every industry from cement plant to grocery store.

Hardening of the arteries may be disastrous for individuals, but it is a wonderful disease for States to contract — if they do their contracting at the right time.

Why Not 'Make Work' for All?

WHEN jobs were short and bread lines were long, one city employed a squad of men to carry stones from one place to another, and a second squad to carry the stones back again. That 'made work' for many men. Other cities stopped using some of their labor-saving machinery on road construction. That also 'made work.'

Why not provide jobs for everybody in this way? If, for example, we suspended the use of telephones in periods of depression, we could set all the idle men and women to work running around with messages.

But, you say, that is absurd. Nobody would stand for such outrageous waste of labor! True. But don't overlook the fact that *all* 'make work' schemes are wastes of labor. They differ only in degree.

Fortunately, they are unnecessary. All we have to do is to plan our needed public works in advance, hold some of them in reserve for emergencies, and have blue prints, specifications, and credit ready for immediate use.

In 1929, we had a dress rehearsal of this plan. It was not a finished performance. Any play is somewhat crude and halting which is put on before the lines are half written, and before the cast of characters has been chosen. This particular production, moreover, was incomplete because Congress — which was engaged in a performance of its own — was slow in providing funds for the scenery. As a matter of fact, Congress never did get around to employing half the required cast. But even this dress rehearsal was enough to demonstrate to a critical audience that it was a real American drama — timely, direct, and profitable.

If States and cities will plan in this way, they will never have to resort to the stupid waste of a 'make work' program.

The Time to Mend Roofs

WHY does the Senate always wait for a new unemployment crisis before even considering measures for preventing unemployment? Chiefly, no doubt, because even Senators are human beings; and Senators, like the rest of us, hate to act unless driven to act.

We all need the spur of catastrophe. It is not vaulting ambition, but calamity, that pricks the sides of our intent. We wait until several hundred prisoners are burned to death before we take adequate fire prevention measures. We wait until ten thousand farms are devastated by the rising waters of the Mississippi before we consider adequate measures for preventing floods.

We take much the same attitude toward the plight of jobless men. When jobs seem plentiful, we are too busy to guard against future trouble. With 'Prosperity' in the headlines, it was not possible to stir up much interest in the Wagner bills to prevent unemployment. They were printed, referred to committees, and promptly buried under an avalanche of 'Prosperity' statistics.

Why bother to oil the engine when the car is running along smoothly at high speed? We don't — not, at least, the intricate and high-powered engine which moves our industrial machinery.

In our neglect of the unemployment problem, we are like the farmer who never did get his roof repaired. When there was rain, he could not mend it; and when the sun shone, there was no need of mending it.

As business revives, there are gains in employment. Headlines about the jobless dwindle. Also bread lines. Then all the papers feature sunshine talks on business. And Congress turns to other things.

Still, the best time to mend roofs is when the sun shines.

Witness Los Angeles!

PROSPERITY came to the United States during the past decade largely by chance. It did not come because organized business foresaw the necessity for a growth of capital expenditures and deliberately planned to bring it about at the right rate. It did not come because the Federal Government exercised such wise leadership of business as it has lately begun to assume.

Nor did prosperity come to our shores because high tariffs prevented Europe from overrunning this country with cheap goods. Most decidedly, prosperity did not come because the people of the United States are a superior race. Other peoples, with equal intelligence and capacity for work, have had no such good fortune.

We have prospered *in the present* by preparing to prosper *in the future*. Witness Los Angeles! How else could such a city have flourished in the desert? Any traveler, crossing the barren wastes of California fifty years ago, could see that no city could ever thrive on that impossible site — on that impossible site where Los Angeles has since been doubling its population every decade!

It was faith in the future — faith made manifest in bricks and steel and cement — that accomplished the impossible. Impelled by that faith, the pioneers went ahead — borrowing money, constructing roads, bridges, schools, hotels, office buildings, warehouses — not for the embryo city which they saw about them, but for the city of their dreams! It was the bold expenditure of enough millions to supply water for a city twice as large, which helped to make that imaginary city a reality.

In laying foundations for a better future, they made the present better than the past.

Pulmotor Ataxia

A DOCTOR pushed his way through the crowd. 'There's a chance for him,' he said. 'Get a pulmotor, quick.'

Some one rushed to a telephone and called the police station. 'Pulmotor,' he gasped. 'Make it snappy.'

The desk sergeant relayed the message. 'Pulmotor,' said the Chief. 'Oh, yes. I'll put in the request. But we can't do anything about it till the next meeting of the Board of Aldermen. Let's see — that comes on the first Tuesday of ——'

The desk sergeant stared. 'Hey, Chief, this feller's most drowned.'

'Rules are rules,' the Chief answered curtly. 'Can't send out a pulmotor without a majority of the Board sign the order. Probably will be more than three weeks,' he speculated.

'But, Chief, this is an emergency. That feller ——'

'That feller,' the Chief interrupted coldly, 'ain't going to hurry up the Board of Aldermen, no matter how drowned he is.'

You don't believe any such conversation ever happened, do you? Well, neither do we. But something very much like it did happen after the stock market crash of 1929. When emergency aid was urged for men out of work, Mr. Hoover recommended that appropriations be made to speed up needed public works.

The recommendation was sent to Congress. There it was provided with comfortable sleeping quarters. Congress then proceeded to discuss obscene literature, lobbies, and wild asses. Several months later, after volume of trade and commodity prices had been falling for six months, Congress began to get ready to take the first steps toward considering the three Wagner bills relating to unemployment, which had been waiting twelve months for attention, and toward thus releasing the unemployment pulmotor.

Why several months? Neither drowning men nor sinking business should be victims of pulmotor ataxia.

Hidden Assets

NO man can realize profits from oil in his back yard until he drills a well. He cannot pay dividends on a summer hotel until there is some way for people to reach it. Hidden assets of this sort are sheer waste.

That is why the people of Spokane are planning to build a parkway along the palisades of the Spokane River, to the now inaccessible Deep Creek Canyon. The whole region is a hidden asset.

That was equally true twenty years ago, of the now world-famed scenes along the Columbia River. Then somebody proposed building the Columbia River Highway.

Of course the idea was condemned as visionary. Those who urged it were supposed to be theorists, unacquainted with the hard facts of business. Still they persisted. They induced three hundred Portland men — community leaders — to take pick and shovel, and begin building the road. Those men discovered something more than protesting muscles, long flabby. They discovered a hidden asset.

Soon a hundred thousand people visited that region who, but for that new road, would never have heard of the beauties of Multnomah Falls. And now, all around the world, whenever any one thinks of Portland, he thinks of the Columbia River Highway and that magnificent gorge 'where rolls the Oregon.'

Ask any Portland citizen to-day what he thinks of spending all that money. He will tell you that all the money has come back, brought from the ends of the earth. And, in addition, Portland has the highway! Those who told the biggest lies about its commercial value told the most truth.

Every other city has hidden assets. In many cases they can be made to yield dividends by the labor of men who would otherwise be idle.

Low Rates Do Not Create Borrowers

THE Federal Reserve Board cannot regulate our tastes. It cannot force us to spend more of our money for some things, and less for other things. It cannot decide for us what is investment and what is speculation, or whether we shall put our savings in banks or in old socks. It cannot prescribe how either individuals or corporations shall spend what money they have.

But the Federal Reserve Board can and does to a large extent determine the total amount of money which is available for circulation — meaning by 'money' both currency and bank credit.

Therein lies great power. The Board can so restrict the supply of money as to raise interest rates for all classes of loans, and slow down building construction. The Board can retard capital development, check the growth of home-building, complicate foreign exchange, and in other ways prevent an adequate flow of money to consumers. Obviously, the Board has sufficient power to bring on an industrial depression.

The Board can use this power, on the basis solely of its own opinion, without the consent or advice of any other body. It is independent of Congress. It does not even have to ask Congress for funds. It is, in fact, the only important branch of the Government over which Congress exercises no control whatever by means of appropriations. The Federal Reserve Board is a law unto itself.

For this reason the Board can act immediately, in an emergency, to increase credit supplies and reduce money rates. This the Board wisely did in 1929 after the stock market crash. Very wisely, the Board then did all that it properly could do, to induce responsible business men to borrow and use more money.

But the Federal Reserve Board cannot *make* anybody borrow money. The Board can make money available. The rest is up to Business.

The Cure for Unemployment

'THE cure for unemployment,' says President Hoover, 'is to find jobs.' Equally evident is the fact that, to find jobs, we need competent agencies which are conducted for that very purpose.

During the War, we acted accordingly. We established Federal Employment agencies, in coöperation with State agencies, to the end that every employable person who was willing to work could find work to do. A good start was made; but it was only a start. Since the War, unhappily, many States have made no progress at all, and some States have lost ground. Says the Director-General of the United States Employment Service: 'In some States, all public employment agencies have ceased to function, because the legislatures have failed to make appropriations. Practically all offices are undermanned, and many are inadequately housed in undesirable locations.'

In spite of this condition of State agencies, the United States Employment Service maintains no employment offices whatever, except those which supply seasonal farm labor.

In the year 1928, these Federal farm labor agencies recruited 541,280 men for seasonal harvesting. That, certainly, was 'curing unemployment by finding jobs.' Does any one doubt that, time and time again, there are 541,280 jobless men, other than farm laborers, who are not within reach of an adequately-manned employment agency?

Mr. Hoover is right: the cure for their trouble is action. But effective action is impossible until we know the location of these men, their training, experience, nationality, and age, as well as the existing demand for, and supply of, each kind of labor in each district. No practical means of keeping such facts constantly available has ever been proposed, except a national system of public labor exchanges.

'The cure for unemployment is to find jobs.'

Doctors of Despair

THE passage by the Senate of Senator Wagner's three bills relating to unemployment marked the end of the Can't-Do-Anything-About-It Economic Policy. One of these bills provides one hundred and fifty million dollars to be expended on certain public works when jobs become scarce. Another bill calls for the regular collection of facts about the unemployed. The third bill sets up a National system of labor exchanges. The three bills are essential parts of a sound, unified program.

The use of more public funds on public works in hard times has been urged over and over again. The plan has been endorsed repeatedly by the American Federation of Labor and by chambers of commerce, and it has been in more than one National party platform.

Still, nothing has ever been done about it. Always there have been too many Doctors of Despair; too many persons who objected to *any* attempt to control fluctuations in business. The *laissez-faire* economics has had too strong a hold. Too many comfortable men have complacently accepted 'hard times' — for other people.

That is why the passage of the Wagner bills was a signal event. A new principle was adopted. Congress declared that the United States Government *can* administer at least part of its expenditures in such a way as to help business in general. That principle is sound.

One hundred and fifty million dollars, to be sure, might not put a large proportion of the unemployed to work, but it would accomplish something. In the future, no doubt, a much larger proportion of the flexible parts of the Federal budget will be administered according to that principle.

The Doctors of Despair might as well stop doubling for the coroner and adopt a cheerful bedside manner.

Buy When Buyers are Scarce

THE American Radiator Company has long helped to keep us from falling upon 'hard times,' and has eased the fall when it did come, for the Company has regularly bought large supplies of pig-iron when there were few buyers in the market, and when business in general needed the stimulus of orders.

Thus the Company has helped producers to keep their furnaces in blast and their wage payments up at times when reduction of wages would have made a bad situation worse.

The action of a few such corporations, if taken before the sag in prices and in employment had gone far, might be enough to check the movement.

In any event, where millions of dollars are involved every month, as in the case of the railroads, the Steel Corporation, General Motors, Sears-Roebuck and Company, and the Telephone Company, right decisions would be strong influences in the right direction.

Often it is a toss-up, in the minds of executives, whether to build a new factory at once or wait a while; whether to order supplies for one month or for several; whether to produce for stock or only for current requirements; whether to declare extra dividends or accumulate surpluses. Often, too, it is an open question whether to do more advertising or less. When such options exist, it would help executives to know which course the general situation calls for.

Corporations, in times of doubt, could decide more wisely what to do in their own cases if they knew more accurately what was doing in the case of business as a whole. The Federal Government should let them know, by furnishing more adequate and more timely information concerning changes in many factors, especially in retail trade, unemployment, stocks on hand, goods in progress, and consumer income.

The Fable of the Two Advertisers

ONCE upon a time, there was a Free-Hearted Advertiser, who used millions of dollars every year to shout his wares. That is to say, every prosperous year.

But the time came when Statistical Boy Scouts, sleuthing around on the horizon for a Business Depression, reported seeing one headed our way. To be sure, it closely resembled Prosperity; but they were smart enough to see through its disguise.

The crash came, as predicted, and buyers hurriedly began getting their dollars in off the street. Those with money in their pockets took it out, counted it, and put it back.

The once-upon-a-time Free-Hearted Advertiser lost nothing but his nerve. That, however, was a total loss. Hastily, he called in his Advertising Dollars and sent out in their place a Squad of Asthmatic Dimes. He was looking out for Number One!

As a sad sequel, Number One now needs looking out for more than ever.

But there was another Advertiser, who was so simple that when leaders of American business, in conference assembled, declared that business was fundamentally sound, he believed them. When sad-eyed retrenchers declared that Prosperity was going to the dogs, he thought he might as well be one of the dogs! So he began barking his wares louder than ever. He knew that buyers are not born, but made. He had found out that the only way to turn the trick is to keep constantly in circulation the word 'buy' and the money with which to buy.

This Advertiser also was looking out for Number One. At the same time, he was giving a much-needed lift to one hundred and twenty million. And the one hundred and twenty million bought. Thus he not only helped to preserve morale, but a good many jobs as well. It paid everybody for this man to advertise.

Old York Teaches New York

NOT long ago, a number of New York factories discharged several thousand workers, without making any effort to find them other work. 'Too bad,' the employers said, 'but there's nothing we can do about it.'

Somehow, that does not sound like resourceful New York. It seems more suitable for Old York. But evidently it isn't. For in that historic English city, where they are still digging up old relics out of the recesses of Roman tombs, they are also digging up new ideas out of the recesses of their own brains.

Rowntree and Company, manufacturers of chocolate, some time ago dug up the idea that employers have a certain responsibility for discharged employees. At once, the Company began to set aside about $50,000 a year out of which to pay benefits to dismissed workers. Later, certain officers of the Company were appointed to give aid to those employees who wished to go into business for themselves.

Recently, when more labor-saving machinery in Rowntree factories threw more men out of work, the Company found, on investigation, that there were no jobs in York for these men. The Company then offered to pay any employer, elsewhere in England, who would take on one of these men, about ten dollars a week for one year, as a contribution toward the cost of training him for the new work.

Even more recently, facing the necessity of discharging more men, the Company found a more durable solution of the problem. After much research, it discovered three industries which promised to provide suitable employment for its discharged workers. Then, using its own capital, it started three small factories. These new units provided new jobs for all Rowntree workers who were displaced by machines.

Let New York go to school to Old York!

'The Elastic Work Day'

WHERE is the worker who has not longed for an Elastic Work Day — one that would contract automatically whenever he felt the urge to play more and work less? But every now and then several million men, with the urge to work more, have thrust upon them another kind of Elastic Work Day — the kind that contracts until there is nothing left of it.

These self-disappearing work days, says President L. F. Loree of the Delaware and Hudson Railroad, can be ruled out by intelligent planning. Witness the success of the Delaware and Hudson. In the business depression of 1930, not one of its employees lost his job.

This achievement came as the result of a sensible and practical 'Elastic Work Day.' The day stretches out toward ten hours when work is unusually heavy. The day contracts toward eight hours when work is not so plentiful. Thus a business depression brings fewer hours, not fewer workers.

This plan reduced the labor turnover from 1450 in 1920, to 172 in 1929 — a reduction of over 88 per cent. In 1920 the difference between the largest number employed in the maintenance branches and the smallest number was 1914. In 1929 the difference was only 418.

'Both the men and the company,' says President Loree, 'benefit by the continuous employment of a group of men educated to its methods and trained to work together. The plan is very popular.'

Much more popular, no doubt, than the explanation still offered to workers by various companies that men lose their jobs periodically 'as a result of natural law,' and nothing can be done about it.

'Years, Idle Years'

I WILL lift up mine eyes unto the hills,' observes bulky G. K. Chesterton, 'but I will not lift my carcass thither.'

Public Opinion has for some time lifted an aspiring eye to the thought of doing something about the 'firing at fifty' nuisance. It is now lifting up its enormous bulk thereto and is actually getting action.

Public Opinion is ex-officio chairman of many ways and means committees, assembled in various industries to consider the high job mortality among the middle-aged. Public Opinion dislikes the spectacle of a fifty-year-old workman forcibly retired to a life of unrestricted leisure and much restricted diet.

So employers whose only question about an employee is 'Can he do the work?' are getting a good deal of deserved publicity. Such publicity is so highly esteemed that we look, any day, to see a sign announcing: 'Plumbing by J. Gazookus. No human hand under fifty touches our bath-tubs.'

Employers who insist that workmen over fifty cannot be profitably retained will soon have to turn in the old alibi. Otherwise Public Opinion will look them over as if they were industrial Rip Van Winkles, and observe scornfully: 'Can't be done profitably! It *is* being done. Look at the Chevrolet Company. It manages to keep a jump or two ahead of the sheriff! Why can't *you?*'

Says the General Manufacturing Manager of the Chevrolet Motor Company: 'We never ask a man's age for the purpose of determining his value to us. In our organization are many men over sixty who are better on the job they are doing than others under forty.'

Other successful companies have also found out that it is safer to measure an employee's value by the worth-days he has ahead, than by the birthdays he has left behind.

'Working Rich Men'

'THE working rich men of America,' says Professor Reed of Columbia, 'have made American workingmen rich.'

Epigrammatic license probably accounts for the second 'rich.' If the American workingman is 'rich,' this is his first notification to that effect. He will not get excited about the news until it is confirmed by his bank account.

Still, there is some truth to Professor Reed's bizarre statement. Certainly the American workingman is better off than he would have been if Owen D. Young, for instance, had retired from industrial life as soon as he had acquired a modest competence.

But it isn't any particular credit to a rich man to refuse to quit a job he loves. It is a serious debit to a workingman to be forced to quit a job he needs.

Leaders of industry, in the last few years, have come to see that there can be no lessening of income to labor, without a resultant lessening of profits to industry. That is only one of the reasons why 'the working rich men of America' are earnestly trying to devise means of sustaining the income of labor.

In the first days of spring, when the boss sits for an hour, staring silently out of his office window, he isn't necessarily dreaming of love, or of his fishing camp in Maine. Oftener than not he is unromantically on the job, blaming himself for laying off men last winter, and trying to figure out how he can avoid doing it next winter.

Most of the men who were invited to the conferences at Washington, after the stock market crash of 1929, were 'working rich men,' but they were also thinking rich men, with the initiative to put their thinking to practical tests.

Such men are helping to make American workingmen, if not rich, at least further from poverty than any other workingmen in the world.

Can Rabbits Climb Trees?

'CO'SE Ah knows no rabbit can climb a tree,' said Uncle Remus, 'but dis time, honey, he just nacherly *had* to.'

Many an industrial company is like the hard-pressed rabbit: under the spur of necessity, it does what it always knew it never could do.

In particular, such companies have found ways, in recent years, of meeting recessions of business without resorting to wage cuts. That is partly because business men have learned, after many expensive lessons, that it is bad business to destroy their own customers.

They have learned, too, that 'liquidation of labor' — the old recourse in time of trouble — is costly in other ways. A business which sacrifices the confidence of employees, in haste of fear, repents at leisure. And spends a lot of money while repenting.

Profiting by these lessons, many concerns keep up their payrolls in spite of a decline in volume of business. Some concerns follow the example of the General Electric Company. Having trained each workman for several jobs, these concerns contrive to keep their employees on the payroll by shifting them from one job to another. Other concerns, following the example of Proctor and Gamble, insure their employees against unemployment; or, following the example of the Dennison Manufacturing Company, they find ways of spreading over twelve months, work which used to be regarded as seasonal. Some of the railroads, under the 'B. and O. Plan,' have found, by consulting their workmen, various means of meeting slack times other than laying off men.

Uncle Remus is right. Nobody knows what he can do until he *has* to.

Those Who Won't Work

LAST spring an Indian knocked at the kitchen door of a ranch house in Nevada, in quest of a hand-out.

'Why, Joe,' said the Rancher, 'I haven't seen you for months. Where are you living now?'

'Me no livin' any more,' grunted the Indian. 'Work all time.'

'Work all the time!' exclaimed the astonished Rancher. 'Where are you working?'

'Oh, mebbe so, me pick potatoes for Pete van Sickle next fall.'

This is the attitude toward labor of a considerable number of unemployed men; and they are not all Indians. They don't want work: they want a hand-out. They could contrive to remain unemployed on a Roman galley. Whatever exertion Industry gets out of them will be sweat wrung from them by 'capitalistic slave drivers.' They think that Industry owes every man a pay envelope. They are not out-and-out loafers. They are willing to go through the motions of earning a living, provided Industry will sit up nights thinking up motions for them to go through.

But Industry is not giving them a thought. The only unemployed men over whose plight Industy is concerned are the men to whom work is not a penalty, but a privilege; the men to whom a job is something more than the worm in the apple of wages.

Industry owes no man a living. All it owes is the opportunity for every man to *earn* a living. It refuses to subsidize shiftlessness; at least, while burglary insurance on the factory clock costs less than paying men to watch it.

The great majority of our unemployed really want to work. They will cease to be unemployed the minute they can get their hands on a job.

Their pay will be earned.

Saving the Shavings

TWO Chinese paupers, man and wife, sat by the roadside when a wealthy merchant passed by, loudly lamenting his recent losses.

'Ah,' cried the woman, 'how happy are we, who have nothing!'

Whereat her spouse, rising and expanding his chest, demanded: 'And to whom, woman, do you owe your fortunate position in life?'

Most of our population have no taxable incomes. To whom do they owe their 'fortunate position in life'?

The capitalist-employer, whose favorite indoor sport was once supposed to be grinding the faces of poor workers, used to be cast for the villain in this tragedy; but now he refuses to play the part, for face-grinding is not a gainful occupation. Nowadays, when employers feel the need of a bit of whittling, they do not begin on wages. Instead, they whittle down production costs, and split the shavings three ways: Part to the workers as wages; another part to the public as lower price of product; and the remainder to capital as profits of increased volume of business. Shavings become savings.

No, the non-taxable income classes do not owe their 'fortunate position' to the capitalist. They owe it to another villain. His name is Ignorance — in this case, Ignorance of the part that money plays in curtailing employment and production. When we wake up to the stupidity of permitting money to cavort at its own sweet will, we shall discover that it is not essentially wayward. It is merely disporting itself in the absence of intelligent orders. When such orders are forthcoming, we shall find that prosperity can be more stable and more equitably distributed.

We shall then have more taxable incomes — more shavings and more savings.

The High Cost of Housing

IT takes a heap of living in a house to make it a home.' But it takes, according to many weary renter-buyers, an even bigger heap of living in one to get it paid for.

The cost of the average small house increased about twenty-five per cent between 1921 and 1928. When last seen, the cost was still soaring. This, says Frederick Keppel, President of the Carnegie Foundation, is absurd. And it is not inevitable.

A better automobile can be bought for five or six hundred dollars to-day than could be bought for twice as much a decade ago. This may account for the bitter complaint of realtors, 'People, at least in summer, fairly live in their cars.'

Executives of sixty building trades associations, representing construction and supply industries, recently recommended the formation of a $500,000 fund to encourage home ownership. We suggest to these executives that the best way to encourage home ownership may be to build better houses and sell them cheaper.

The automobile industry found ways to cut costs, increase wages, improve the product, and sell more of it. Doubtless the construction industry can do the same thing. This is a good time in which to make a start. Money for building purposes is cheaper than it has been for years.

Four thousand scientists are employed in the laboratories of the American Telephone and Telegraph Company. Their function is to find ways of perfecting service and reducing costs to consumers. The construction industry needs more research.

'Home,' says Robert Frost, 'is the place where, when you have to go there, they have to let you in.' It shouldn't be a place where, when you have to build one, the builder, because of antiquated methods, is forced to *take* you in.

Most people want to own permanent homes. But they don't like homes with permanent-mortgage trimmings.

Our Common Enterprise

A NUMBER of industrial companies have set up relations between employer and employee which give promise of an end of the old conflict between labor and capital. A case in point is the Standard Oil Company of New Jersey.

From many such experiments, it is now clear that, instead of the future promising no more than a drawn battle, there is ground for hope of a common effort in industry, based on the true principle of a common enterprise. This principle demands that the employer shall not, at any time, force upon the employee wages, hours, and working conditions, merely because he has, at the time, the economic power to do so.

In our day, most workmen *must* be employed in order to live. Production by means of costly factories and tools makes this necessary. If a man is experienced and trained, he is often dependent upon a particular industry, sometimes a particular plant. This is especially true if he owns his home, or is otherwise established in a community.

At times, there are many seekers for every job. At such times, the employer has a great economic advantage. The employer should not seize it. At any time, for any company, there is a fair wage that can be paid, if *any* wage can be paid. The conditions in the company, in the industry, and general business conditions determine this wage. Sometimes it is higher, sometimes lower; but whatever it is, it is not to be determined by the amount for which men would work rather than not to work at all. This is equally true of hours of labor and other conditions of work. These are questions of fact, to be determined as such.

Labor and capital are in the right frame of mind to deal with such questions when they look upon their efforts as a common enterprise.

'Collective Bargaining'

WHAT affects a man's very livelihood — and the bread and shoes and shelter of his children — should not be the subject of bargaining. Most men have no alternative except to work for what they can get. When a man *must* sell, and this fact is known, there can be no true bargain. More and more, in all branches of business, where the buyer and seller are not equally free, the tendency is away from so-called 'bargaining' and toward prices that are fair under the conditions.

'Collective bargaining' rests upon the false assumption that employer and employees are free to reach an agreement or not. With conditions in industry as they are, 'collective bargaining' necessarily relies on economic pressure by employer, or employees, or both. Fair wages, hours, and working conditions cannot be determined by bargaining.

In different companies, these questions of fact have been determined in different ways. The method of the Standard Oil Company of New Jersey is one of the most democratic and one of the simplest. A similar method is in use by the General Electric Company. Other methods are the so-called Leitch plan and the 'Industrial Republic' of the Goodyear Tire and Rubber Company. Various other plans are more or less successfully accomplishing the same purpose.

It is important in this connection to bear in mind that wages are part of the cost of production. Moreover, selling prices are influenced by this cost; and what wages will buy is determined by these selling prices. Great fluctuations in wages and great fluctuations in prices go hand in hand and have harmful consequences. This makes it important that economic pressure should not determine wages, hours, and working conditions.

Is It Safe to Work?

ONE and one half million years may not seem a long time to the newly discovered planet. For all we know, that may be merely the years of its adolescence. But one and one half million years seems a long time to us.

Anyway, it is too much time to waste. Yet, according to the Travelers' Insurance Company, adults in the United States waste fully as much time as that every year on account of accidents. Motor vehicle accidents alone last year caused the death of five times the number killed in both armies during the battle of Gettysburg. Year in and year out, as a matter of fact, the casualties in the battlefields of industry exceed those of war.

The losses of war loom large only at times, but the losses of accidents pile up with frightful regularity. A mine explosion yesterday, a broken scaffold to-day, a train wreck to-morrow: every day ticks off its quota. In part, we are buying our industrial ascendancy at the price of limbs and lives.

The time lost last year by persons hurt in occupational mishaps, when computed at the average wage income, represents more than a billion dollars. Not only were these accidents the direct cause of physical and economic harm to the victims; but indirectly they affected the welfare of all of us.

Are these industrial accidents necessary? Not at all necessary, says Professor Edison L. Bowers. They are preventable, he insists, in at least 75 per cent of the cases. And he has written a book to prove it. The book is called *Is It Safe To Work?*

Professor Bowers proposes definite, practical measures for preventing accidents, and for reducing the labor-time lost on account of accidents which are not preventable. He does not use his professorial right to theorize. He stays on rock bottom. He shows how to prevent the loss of at least a million years out of the Travelers' computed one and a half million, to say nothing of the painful hours in bed that *seem* like a million years.

'Curiouser and Curiouser'

WHEN we were very young and insisted on knowing about everything, they used to tell us that 'curiosity killed a cat.'

Well, it never kills business men. If it did, the mortality would be terrific, for there is no limit to the things business men are getting curious about.

Three years ago, the Metropolitan Life Insurance Company got curious about labor turnover. It began to gather and compile statistics on the expenses of that troublesome pair, Hire and Fire. It found out that fifty dollars was the average hiring-firing cost. Then Uncle Sam took over the job, and now there is published at Washington — accessible to every one — a monthly index of labor turnover.

This index enables the curious manufacturer to check up on his own hiring-firing record and find out its relation to the national average. If it is above the average, and his curiosity holds out, he can find out why, and cut down his own turnover costs. If his average is lower than the national average, he may contribute helpful hints to Uncle Sam. And Uncle Sam, in his rather new capacity as Business Leader, is not too proud to accept hints from all his up-and-coming nephews.

The cat that curiosity killed was probably curious about something that wasn't any of its business. But labor — if you are an employer — decidedly *is* your business.

It costs you money, going and coming. Fifty dollars, on the average, per go-and-come.

Get curious. Send for a Government labor-turnover index. Put to work the head that built up your business, and devise ways of cutting down your turnover costs.

'Shut Up' or 'Open Up'?

THE sour-faced foreman who used to growl 'shut up' at chatty workmen is going out. The new model will say, politely, 'open up.' He will actually invite his men to talk. What is more, he will listen attentively to what they have to say.

This technique has increased production at the Western Electric Company's Chicago plant 35 per cent.

So, at last, the psychoanalysts have run into real competition. Why pay those lofty practitioners lofty prices for the privilege of pouring out to them your concealed yearnings? How much more satisfactory to get a job with the Western Electric Company and 'yearn while you earn.'

It is mentally stifling, the psychoanalysts have been telling us, to put away your grievances in moth balls. Take the ornery things out and give them the air. A musty Grievance develops into a Repression. A Repression, as soon as it gets of age, becomes an Emotional Explosion.

The Western Electric idea seems to be to catch a Grievance young, treat it kindly, and encourage it to tell everything. This forestalls Emotional Explosions. And among factory owners, there is next to no demand for explosions of any kind.

Successfully to air a Grievance, however, requires something more than air. This 'something' is a Sympathetic Listener.

Well, what has all this to do with economics? A great deal. It has so much to do with production and morale that this progressive company, on the 'sympathetic listening' motif, is recasting its whole system of employment. It has formulated a new plan for interviewing each of its forty thousand employees. Instead of replacing foremen by mechanical supervisors, it has found a way to replace mechanical supervisors by human beings. This ought to be enough to make almost any one a Western Electric fan.

'He Never Had a Chance'

THE man who complains that 'he never had a chance' should not be set down as a liar, even in this Land of Opportunity. He may be speaking the truth. Possibly he never observed that chances are shy young things, brought up to sit tight until grabbed. He never did *have* a chance. He never *took* one!

Only the bold deserve the fair chance. And what is more, only the bold get it.

The man who yearns for 'better business' will do well to face the full implication of that first syllable. The way to get 'better business' is to bet on it. If the word 'risk' has a holier ring in his ears, he is free to use it. But bet he must, and does.

Even when he goes into a panic-stricken huddle and does nothing, he bets. He bets that inactivity will win. He places his bet on the black outlook, and it turns up red — in the ledger.

No man needs to bet recklessly. He is entitled to all the facts that will help him to bet wisely. The more facts, the better the bet. But in the end he must act, and act without guarantee of results. Like Abraham, he must go out, not knowing whither he goeth.

We owe our huge industries, not to men who counted the cost, but to men who discounted it; men who scorned to sidle along in the trough of the wave, but headed straight into the storm, and took the impact head on.

It takes big men to go ahead when the rank and file are hanging back. It takes big men to place orders when cowards are cancelling orders.

We need more big men. Men who wouldn't bet a bent collar button on the platitude that 'all things come to him who waits.' Men who would bet their last dollar on the truth that all things come to the man who knows when to go ahead!

There is one way to make American Prosperity: Bet on it.

Non-Stop Dollars

WILLIAM CULLEN BRYANT KEMP, A.M., M.D., LL.B., LL.M., B.S., PH.D., C.E., E.E., Mech. E., Phar. Chem., who died at the age of 78, held the world's endurance record for college students. He went to college all his life.

This non-stop student had the passion of the collector. But instead of collecting bits of orange peel, as did the great Doctor Johnson, Doctor Kemp collected college degrees.

The reason he pursued knowledge to the grave is simple. When he was a very young man, a will provided that he should receive $2500 a year 'as long as he remains in school.' Thereafter, upon each Commencement Day for sixty years, this young man found it easier to remain in school and accumulate knowledge than to go out into the cold, cold world, and try to accumulate $2500 a year.

What did he do with this vast store of knowledge? Nothing at all.

He became a doctor of medicine, but he did not heal the sick.

He became an engineer, but he built no bridges.

He became a master of arts, but the only art he practiced was that of hoarding knowledge and locking it up in the safe deposit vaults of his mind.

He had time to read everything that deserved to be written, but he wrote nothing that deserves to be read.

We look with contempt on such a piling up of sterile learning. Some day we shall look with equal contempt on those misers who collect dollars, only in order that they may collect more dollars; who lock them up most securely at the very time when business languishes and lays off men, for want of dollars spent.

Some day we shall have more non-stop dollars and, consequently, more non-stop jobs.

He Who Knocked at Your Door

A MAN knocked at your door. He wanted work. He wanted to cut your wood. You had plenty of wood to be cut; but you were too smart just to hand him an ax and tell him to go to it. First, you had to find out about him.

So you asked questions. You learned that without work on your woodpile the man had no means of support. That classified him. He was a vagrant.

When you learned that, you felt better. Now you knew exactly what to do with him.

First, you led him to a small room and locked him in. This was to make sure he would not annoy other people who had woodpiles.

Next, you put aside some money to be used in feeding him. You had to take it out of money which might have been used toward a new playground for the children. But vagrants must be fed.

Next, you built a house to put him in. That cost more money. But vagrants must be sheltered.

By this time your caller, obsessed by the delusion that he wanted to split your wood, began to yell for an ax. Then you knew he was dangerous, so you hired an attendant. That cost more money. But vagrants must be guarded.

Along about this time you woke up. 'I declare,' you said peevishly, 'when I figure up what all this feeding and sheltering and guarding has cost, I wish I had handed him an ax in the first place and been done with it. It would have been cheaper to let him split the blamed wood!'

You say this never happened to you? No? Well it did happen to some member of your family.

Maybe it was your Uncle Sam.

National Life Insurance Day

A LITTLE while ago, we celebrated 'National Own a Home Day.' This was followed by 'National Eat an Apple Day.' Then came 'National Life Insurance Day.' Some time, perhaps, we shall all give a sigh of relief while we celebrate 'National Leave People Alone Day.' Still, we might have done worse with a day than to dedicate it to life insurance.

As a matter of fact, the year 1929 will go down, in the history of thrift, as the year in which our persistent agents actually lifted the total life insurance in force in the United States to one hundred billion dollars. And that is more than our national annual income.

How fast we have moved lately toward the security which comes from savings! Although it took us eighty years to pile up the first fifty billions of life insurance, it took only seven years for the next fifty billions.

As for the *per capita* increase in savings during the last half century, it is difficult to believe the statistics. While the population increased scarcely more than two-fold, bank deposits increased twenty-five-fold, and life insurance fifty-fold. Evidently, we did not put all our savings into the stock market.

Life insurance is now an important factor in the growing stability of trade and employment, for it helps to sustain consumer purchasing power. Each year about one and three quarter billion dollars is received by policy holders and beneficiaries. Each year life insurance is responsible for about 87 per cent of the estates that are left.

Evidently life insurance is not only 'the first line of defense against poverty,' but it is also one of the chief means of stabilizing the buying of millions of consumers, thus helping to prevent violent trade fluctuations.

166

'With All She Earns on Her Back'

S HE puts all she earns on her back!' This horrified criticism of the working girl breaks out every day. At least, unlike some of her critics, the working girl *does* earn her raiment. She doesn't chain some unsuspecting male to a galley and put all *he* earns on her back.

Deciding what *other* women can afford is a pastime for women of leisure. But while these self-appointed reformers are working out to five decimal places what the working girl can afford, the working girl goes ahead and settles that problem for herself.

She is ready to put her shoulder to the wheel; but she insists that it shall be a well-tailored shoulder. She will stand for a day's work that would prostrate her critic, but she refuses to stand for it in shabby shoes. Having no income from bonds with which to buy a wardrobe, she earns it herself. Having no maid to take care of it, she takes care of it herself — after hours.

She has won a battle in the war against poverty. She deserves to be decorated, and she sees to it that she *is.*

Now that we have worked up a case for the defendant, we take pleasure in announcing that there *isn't* any defendant. The indictment has been quashed by the findings of the Business Girls' Budget Contest, conducted by the Exposition of Women's Arts and Industries. The accused are not guilty, as charged; at least, not in New York, and probably not elsewhere. They spend on clothes only 25 per cent of what they earn.

And the result! That, in itself, is an 'exposition of women's arts and industries.'

After all, the point is this: Nowhere in the world do people rise to higher standards of living until they *want* to rise. It is fully to the credit of wage-earning girls that they want to dress well, and industry is fully equipped to dress them well.

Our Saving Grace

ANOTHER illusion shattered! No sooner had we recovered from the shock of learning that working girls do not put all they earn on their backs, when 'lo, from out vacuity another incongruity!' Workingmen do not put all their spare change into spark plugs, radio tubes, and silk shirts. They put a substantial chunk of wages into assuring the *next* generation of plenty of spark plugs and radio tubes, or their next-generation equivalent.

To this commendable end, workers buy insurance. More than 67 million persons — more than half the total population — are insured. Thirty years ago, life insurance companies in the United States collected a paltry four hundred million dollars. This year they will collect four thousand million dollars. Industrial policies alone have increased in number from about eleven million to about ninety million.

This is the very period during which wage-earners have increased their ownership of automobiles from about fifteen to about fifteen million. While the workingman has been buying automobiles, radios, better homes, and better clothes, he has been investing more and more money in insurance policies, bank accounts, bonds, and stocks.

The more he spends, the more he saves. He saves more, not in spite of the fact that he spends more, but because of it.

More spending means more business. More business means higher wages. Higher wages make more buyers and more savers.

Two billion dollars will be paid this year by insurance companies to policyholders in the United States and their beneficiaries — consumers all. The luxury-loving recipients will use this money to buy radios, automobiles, fur coats, and Spanish villas, not to mention bread and bonds.

And more insurance policies.

Spend-Thriftiness

A SIGN in a suburban bank lures depositors thus: 'Some one will save the money you spend. Why not save it yourself?'

That is one of those convenient records which can be played either side up. Whenever trade is dull and jobs are scarce, we like *this* side: 'Some one will spend the money you save. Why not spend it yourself?'

The money you save will be used by somebody to finance production. But production has no trouble in getting itself financed.

The money you spend for goods finances consumption. At times consumption does have trouble in getting itself financed.

The money you save may be used to produce goods, which may or may not be sold. The money you spend certainly will move the goods already made and create a demand for more.

A demand for goods is potentially a demand for labor. A demand for labor means more wages for consumers. And more wages for consumers — provided consumers' goods increase at the same rate — mean higher standards of living.

A nation which reduces its spending when millions of men are idle is wasting its substance in riotous saving.

When business has had a setback, it takes time for it to change gears and get set to go forward. Often, it requires months for new construction projects to get out of the blue prospect stage into the blue print stage. It takes more months to run the obstacle race from blue prints to blue overalls.

During these blue months, all the money you can *prudently* spend will do you no harm, and will do good to jobless men somewhere.

By all means, 'save for a rainy day.' But don't think you are thereby speeding up business.

To speed up business, buy an umbrella.

Spending in the Rain

WE do not spend money very freely when business skies are cloudy, even those of us who have plenty of money to spend. We can't buy This. We can't buy That. We are saving for a Rainy Day.

Of course the Rainy Day arrives. The floods descend and the markets fall.

Then what happens? Do we fetch forth the best galoshes and slay the fatted bankroll? We do not. We go without some more of This and some more of That. We start saving for a Rainier Day.

All we have to do at any time is to keep on saving hard enough, and the Rainier Day will arrive. It can't help itself.

We hate to spend money on the Rainy Day we saved it for! We hate to do anything on a rainy day except, perhaps, listen on the radio to 'Singing in the Rain.' But let the Chamber of Commerce orchestra strike up 'Spending in the Rain,' and most of us don't even recognize the tune!

Yet a dollar saved for a Rainy Day is merely a dollar saved.

A dollar spent on a Rainy Day is a dollar earned, and spent again, and so on, till the cows come home.

When business activity is 10 per cent below normal, as it was in the winter of 1929–30, industry resorts to many expedients, old and new, in order to provide Rainy Day jobs, and the Government appropriates millions to speed up its Rainy Day Building Program.

But it is precisely at such a time that many of us hang on to our Rainy Day Dollar, as if double pneumonia would get it the moment it touched a foot to the damp ground. We intend to take it out for an airing some day, but not till the sun shines. We prefer to spend it when business doesn't need it.

The sun will shine some day, but not until the Rainy Day Dollar steps out.

Jack Dullboy's Aim in Life

SUPPOSE Jack works forty years and saves his money —
like a good boy — and then goes to his bank and says:
'I'm sick of saving. I'm sick of working. I have no dependents.
I have saved enough money to last me. Please let me have it
all. Now I want to play.'

Picture the dismay on the face behind the brass grill!

'For twenty years,' says Professor Bennett in the *Yale Review*, 'the bank might have been telling me that saving was for
my children or for my old age; yet now, when I took it at its
word, the establishment would have a collective apoplexy.

'Why? Not merely because it would lose some money that it
might have invested with profit to itself, but chiefly because
to a banker the idea of spending money for enjoyment is a sort
of sacrilege. Money, in his philosophy, is not to be spent, but
to be saved. Capital is to breed interest; interest is to be added
to capital, which is in turn to produce more interest, and so on,
and so on. Far away on the horizon of progress, he sees a perfect Everest of capital soaring into the inane. Sublime spectacle!

'Yes, but what will he do with it?

'The ideal of a banker is Work. Mine is Enjoyment. If
I save, it is in order that I may spend; if I work, it is in order
that I may enjoy the fruits of my labor. The ideal of work for
work's sake seems to me stupid, inhuman, and, above all,
dull.'

Thanks be! Here is a professor *any one* can understand.

Virtue may be its own reward, but thrift isn't. What is the
use of piling up savings if it is always going to be wicked to
enjoy them?

All work and no play makes Jack a dull boy.

Guilt-Edge Insecurities

UNEMPLOYMENT in the winter of 1929–30 cost us — you and me and all the rest of us — much less than it might have cost us. That was because a lot of little dollars went to market.

But unemployment cost us a lot more than it should have cost us. That was because too many little dollars stayed at home.

Many of the little dollars that went to market were corporation dollars. They knew where they were going, and how important it was to get there in a hurry.

Many of the little dollars that stayed at home were family dollars. They had scruples about going to market on a rainy day.

The little dollars that went to market got busy and made jobs.

The little dollars that stayed at home got sleeping sickness and made trouble.

The little corporation dollars that went to market had various motives. Some of them were soldiers going to the front. Some of them went because they wanted to be where there was something going on. Some of them went because they believed Mr. Hoover knew what he was talking about when he asked them to go.

But whatever their motives, they all made jobs!

Some family dollars went to market, too; some for no higher motive than 'keeping up with the Joneses.' But even these low-minded dollars made jobs. The only dollars that made trouble were the ones that hung back with the Groanses.

The little dollars we send promptly to market, when markets are low in spirits, bring us gilt-edge economic securities. The little dollars we keep fearfully at home at such times net us guilt-edge insecurities.

Riotous Saving

SAVED money is of no use to the country as a whole until it is invested. But it is useless to invest money in more mills, mines, and machines than the country can use; and usually the country has more than it can use.

Once any nation has piled up larger savings in the form of capital facilities than the nation can operate, there is virtually no way in which it can save anything more to advantage. It can merely accumulate more idle capital facilities — and more 'No Men Wanted' signs.

The thrifty individual, to be sure, who saves five dollars instead of buying a pair of shoes, *may* be better off for his thrift. What are savings for an individual, however, are not necessarily savings for society. Every one who saves money at times when his abstinence helps to curtail production and throw men out of work, saves at the expense of other people.

For the individual, a penny saved is a penny earned; but for society, a penny saved is sometimes a penny lost.

This, then, is the Dilemma of Thrift: both producers and consumers *must* save; but there are times when they do not save without to some extent frustrating the social object of saving.

The country can use more invested savings — more instruments of production — only if consumers spend more money. But in 1929–30 the fact that commodity prices fell off for a full year, while production and car-loadings fell off, too, showed that for a full year consumers had not been spending enough money to enable producers to keep their plants running. The monster penny-in-the-slot machine had not been clicking fast enough.

When, under such conditions *wealthy* people *save* more money, they are wasting the substance of the country in riotous saving.

Does Lavish Spending Help the Poor?

'SPARE no expense in making the wedding as simple as possible.' That was the only direction which the bride's father gave for a recent Fifth Avenue wedding. No expense was spared. The 'beautiful simplicity' of the wedding was described in detail by newspapers everywhere. It cost approximately $110,000.

Are such expenditures a benefit to the poor? That sum was a favorite subject for debate in the lyceums of a generation ago. As an argument in favor of lavish buying, the point was always made that the more money the rich spend, the more jobs there are for the poor. One wedding at $110,000 means the greater part of $110,000 paid to engravers, cooks, waiters, policemen, jewelers, florists, musicians, dressmakers, and all the rest. But the speakers for the negative in the old Lyceum days always replied that the poor would be better off if their labor were used to produce necessities instead of orchids and ribbons. There the debate usually ended. No convincing conclusion was ever reached.

The fact is, no satisfactory answer to the question can be found, without taking into account the status of trade and employment. When commodity prices are weakening, and jobs are becoming scarcer, lavish expenditures by the rich certainly do help the poor. The poor are better off making luxuries, and enjoying the luxury of steady pay, than having no pay at all.

When, on the other hand, sales are outrunning production, prices are rising, and labor is scarce, the outlay of one hundred thousand dollars for a wedding only makes the situation worse. It helps create a vicious spiral of inflation. And from inflation the poor suffer more than the rich.

If the rich must compete in expenditures for weddings, yachts, gardens, and wardrobes, let them spare no expense in making their extravagance as timely as possible.

Saving Dollars and Divorces

ON National Budget Day, we are reminded of the almost incredible fact that Uncle Sam used to spend his billions without a budget. The method was simple. Every day he spent what he pleased. Then, when he got around to it, he had somebody figure out the deficit, and ordered you and all the rest of us to pay it.

That method might do for your own household, if you could order your income increased every time you ran short of money. But you wouldn't get your money's worth. Uncle Sam never did. Nobody does. Extemporaneous spending, without reference to what was spent yesterday or to what must be spent tomorrow, is confusing to a bank account, and often causes it to lose its balance.

It is always economical to know where you are going, and to have some means of telling how far you have gone. On the highway it saves gasoline and tires. On the railroad it saves cars and passengers. In the home it saves dollars and divorces.

Saving money, instead of spending it, is what most people mean by thrift. That kind of thrift is usually good for the individual, but it is not always good for society.

But the kind of thrift which means budgeting household expenditures prudently over fifty-two weeks of every year is always good — good both for the family and for the nation. It helps to stabilize trade and employment.

By the use of a budget, Uncle Sam now saves a million dollars here and a million dollars there. By the same method, any housewife can save a dollar here and a dollar there — which means as much to her as a million dollars mean to her Uncle Sam.

A budget, rightly used, assures her a little money on hand whenever she most needs it, and more for her money whenever she spends it.

A Word to the Wife

TWENTY-FOUR million purchasing agents in the United States are not as shrewd as they might be in spending their billions. Such is the finding of a recent survey. But since these purchasing agents are only housewives, they probably will not lose their jobs.

The chief count against them is that they are not as good judges of quality as their grandmothers were. They depend upon trade-marks and cost. They seem to think that 'the higher the price, the better is the article.'

This, it appears, is not always the case. The Department of Economics of the University of Cincinnati tested silk stockings priced from $1.50 to $2.95, and found that the $1.50 grade were of better quality than all but one of the more expensive grades.

It is probably true that women to-day are not as good judges of quality as were their grandmothers. When grandmother was given a dollar to spend, she never knew when, where, or if, she would be trusted with another. Of course she was a judge of durability. She had to be, or move to the South Sea Islands!

Our guess is that every male head of a family who reads this page will show it to his wife.

His smile will say, 'I told you so.'

She will say, 'Bosh,' and calmly change the subject.

But the next morning, when the wise husband himself is selecting theater tickets on the assumption that the highest price indicates the best show, his purchasing-agent spouse will be up and doing. She will be at the stocking counter in her favorite store. Handing the salesman a small package, she will make the following speech — and she will make it with an air of calm authority: 'Please credit these $2.95 stockings, and show me your $1.50 brand, which is just as good, if not better!'

Nerve and Noise

HOW much flattery do we, as customers, require at the hands of merchants; and what, in cold cash, are we willing to pay for it? Suppose all the retail stores at which we have charge accounts were to add to our bill, 'Flattery charge, one dollar.' Would we pay it without protest? Is it worth a dollar a month — or any other sum a month — to know that no matter how noisy or nervous or whimsical we may be, we are, as customers, 'always right'?

As a matter of fact, to the extent that we are swayed by cupidity and whims, we are *not* always right, no matter how many merchants believe it is good business to tell us that we are. The buyer, like the seller, is entitled to courtesy and full value for his money. To the extent that he demands and gets more — more attention, more concessions, more value in time or goods than reasonable customers ask — he is responsible for waste for which we *all* pay.

'Let the buyer beware' has gone into the dust-heap of policies which have outlived even their imaginary usefulness. It never was good business. Neither is its paradoxical twin, 'The customer is always right.'

Some one should pay the merchant for time and money lost because of demands by unreasonable customers. Why not send the bill to them? Why expect those of us who wear a coat only once before we bring it in for exchange, to pay the freight for the hardy souls who wear a coat a week and then indignantly deny that it was ever unwrapped?

Neither courteous merchants nor their reasonable customers should subsidize *noise* and *nerve*.

The Quantity Theory of Money

EVERY one knows that with a given quantity of money he can buy and pay for a given quantity of goods, at given prices, *and no more.*

(By money we mean, of course, currency of all kinds, as well as checks on bank deposits.)

What is true of each of us, individually, is true of all of us, put together.

This means that in the United States, in any one year, the volume of goods that can be bought and paid for, without a fall in the price-level, is determined by the quantity of money in ʌiation and the average number of times the money is used to pay for goods. Other factors remaining the same, more goods cannot be sold unless there is more money in circulation. When the money in circulation is reduced, the volume of trade must be reduced, or the price-level must fall.

That is one statement of the much discussed Quantity Theory of Money. It is true absolutely. It is true of long periods of time and short periods. It is not a subject for argument. There is as much ground for challenging the truth of the equation: 2×6 equals 3×4.

This does not tell us whether falling prices are caused by decreases in the volume of money, or decreases in the volume of money are caused by falling prices. But for our chief practical purposes, we do not need to know.

What we *do* need to know, when business lags, is how we can stop the fall in the commodity price level and regain our lost volume of trade and employment. The Quantity Theory of Money gives us an essential part of the answer.

In the depression of 1930, one of our business leaders said to the President: 'I don't know whether you believe in the Quantity Theory of Money. I don't know whether I do. But there is no hope for a revival of business unless we do.'

In the Laboratory and in Life

OTHER things remaining equal, business falls off in exact proportion to the falling off of money in circulation. That is in accord with the Quantity Theory of Money.

But at once the objection arises that other things *never do* remain equal. The objection is valid. For that reason, dollar volume of business does not rise and fall in absolutely fixed relation to the rise and fall of money in circulation. Nevertheless, the relation is so close that a change in the quantity of money is plainly the dominant factor in price inflation.

In any given year, to be sure, many other factors also change. The practical business man, however, does not, for that reason, impatiently brush aside the Quantity Theory of Money. He is aware that no theory works out in life exactly as it works out in a laboratory.

Take the Law of Supply and Demand, for example. Business men believe in it devoutly. Some one has said, 'Teach a parrot to say Supply and Demand, and you have made a business man.' According to this 'Law,' the price of a given commodity goes up whenever the demand increases faster than the supply; and vice versa.

Yet every business man knows of cases in which *increased* demand has resulted in *decreased* prices; automobiles, for example. And he knows of many widely advertised specialties which sell for the same price, year in and year out, regardless of changes in demand. Nevertheless, the business man remains convinced of the practical importance of the Law of Supply and Demand. He is right.

For the same reason, he is right in attaching great weight to the Quantity Theory of Money. Although other factors play their part and never do remain equal, the business man observes that a change in the quantity of money is always the largest factor in trade fluctuations.

Is Economics an Exact Science?

THE lay reader accepts the statement of bacteriologists that they have found five million germs on the blade of a knife, though he hasn't the slightest idea how anybody counts five million germs.

The lay reader accepts the findings of such men because he supposes that they are dealing with exact sciences. He is more wary about anything that economists have to say, because the 'social sciences' are not exact sciences.

As a matter of fact, there are *no* exact sciences. Measurements in physics, for example, are only approximately accurate. The engineer is so wary of his own measurements of the strength of materials that he designs bridges to stand several times the maximum load.

Many measurements in economics are sufficiently exact for everyday use. By means of index numbers, economists now record changes in the purchasing power of money, for example, with an instrumental error that rarely exceeds one part in 800. That amounts to an error of one cent in an eight dollar expense account, or one pound in the weight of a horse. For most practical purposes, such an error is negligible.

The accuracy of economic studies was strikingly shown when the National Bureau of Economic Research completed two wholly independent studies of the national income. The two studies, carried on for years by separate staffs, were based on different methods and different sources. They involved millions of computations. Yet, at the end, the findings were very much the same.

Our chief trouble is not our inability to measure the forces which make for good business and full employment, but our failure to use the available means of measurement. It is as easy to count five million unemployed workers as to count five million germs.

Whose Prosperity?

READING every day about the amazing prosperity of the United States, many of us are prompted to ask, 'Whose prosperity?' Do the gains go chiefly to those who are wise enough, or lucky enough, to get in and out of the stock market at the right time? Or do the wage-earners have a substantial share of this 'amazing prosperity'?

These questions are answered in a book on 'Real Wages' by Dr. Paul H. Douglas, Professor of Industrial Relations at the University of Chicago. It is the outcome of eight years of research; and the conclusions are based on no fewer than three million computations.

Professor Douglas finds that the cost of living is 135 per cent above that of the closing decade of the last century. He finds, however, that dollar wages in all manufacturing industries have risen 215 per cent. This means that real wages, in the present century, have risen about 34 per cent. In other words, workers in manufacturing industries can now buy with their wages four units of goods, for every three units they could buy in the decade, 1890–99.

The gains have been well distributed among industries. The range is from 17 per cent gained by leather workers to 46 per cent gained by non-ferrous metal workers. Between these extremes come the employees in the food, textile, clothing, iron, lumber, printing, glass, and land vehicles industries. Unskilled laborers, with a gain of 32 per cent since 1914, have fared almost as well as workers in manufacturing concerns. Railroad workers have not fared so well. They have gained only 22 per cent. In the years just before the stock market crash, real wages in manufacturing concerns were increasing at a rapid rate.

In answer, therefore, to the question, 'Whose prosperity?' all classes of labor have reason to reply, 'My prosperity.'

Incomes Up Fifty-Five Per Cent

MAN does not live by bread alone. Neither does he live by bread, cake, gasoline, radios, and all the other things which he buys with his wages. The average worker in our manufacturing concerns can now buy about 35 per cent more than he could buy before the War. But that is not the whole story. A part of his *income* has not been *wages*.

Every worker enjoys *free income* through various forms of public service. He receives, for example, free fire, police, and health protection, as well as free facilities for education and recreation. Of late, State and local government expenditures for such purposes have increased greatly. In 1890, they were only $8.44 per capita; in 1924, $62.35. To-day, they are still higher. The Federal Government also has increased its appropriations for welfare purposes, principally for highways which are used by everybody. Account should be taken, as well, of the greatly increased private contributions to charitable and educational agencies.

Even that is not all. Wage-earners have made further gains through industrial benefit systems, accident compensations, and payments of various sorts to veterans of the late War. Still further gains in real income per family have resulted from a decrease in the average number of persons dependent on each wage-earner, and a decrease in the volume of unemployment.

Professor Paul H. Douglas concludes that, between 1890–99 and 1926, the real income of wage-earners increased 55 per cent. This includes:

Gain in real wages....................	35 per cent
Gain in free incomes.................	7 per cent
Gain through decreased unemployment..	8 per cent
Gain through fewer dependents........	5 per cent

Why Have Real Wages Gone Up?

WHAT is the cause of the remarkable increase in real wages? At bottom, the cause is increased productivity of labor. Real wages, during the past forty years, made no gains precisely in those years when productivity per worker made no gains. The largest gains all came in the very years —namely, 1919 to 1929 — in which the largest gains were made in the output per worker.

How has this increased productivity come about ?

Mainly through the progress of science. If one laborer to-day, with labor-saving devices and electric power, can do one hundred times more work than one primitive man, it is because to-day every laborer has, in effect, one hundred slaves working for him.

Another cause of the increase in real wages has been the decrease in the rate of growth of the labor supply. This decrease has been caused by the falling-off in immigration and in the birthrate.

Still further to account for the gains in the wages of manufacturing workers, we must note the fact that the exchange value of farm products has not risen as rapidly as the exchange value of manufactured goods. Industrial centers have made their gains partly at the expense of the farm population.

Finally, workers have been more efficient since prohibition went into effect. It is impossible to measure the part, if any, which prohibition has had in the increased well-being of wage-earners; but there is no escape from the fact that the substantial increase in real wages began in 1917, when prohibition laws and war-time restrictions actually did reduce the sales of liquor.

The most important point to remember is that wages have gone up during the past fifteen years, mainly because production has gone up. And if wages go up during the next fifteen years, it will be mainly for the same reason.

'Where Wealth Accumulates'

ABOUT two hundred thousand travelers from the United States in the past twelve months, we estimate, have heard their country referred to as a land 'where wealth accumulates and men decay.' So-called American Prosperity, says one of these critics, is 'a flashy thing.'

Are these caustic critics right? What, after all, is this 'so-called American prosperity'?

First of all, it consists of better health. The years of suffering have been reduced; the years of life, lengthened.

Second, it consists of increased production.

Third, the share of wage-earners in the national income has grown faster than the share of property owners.

Fourth, we must list other economic gains — life insurance, for example. It took us eighty years to accumulate the first fifty billions; seven years for the next fifty. Add to this the gains in accident, health, and employment insurance, in pensions and in bank deposits, and the gains of wage-earners in stock and bond ownership, and we have evidence — in spite of the inexcusable curse of unemployment — of increased economic security.

'That, however,' replies the foreign critic, 'is merely evidence of richer bank accounts, not of richer human beings. It tells us nothing about participation in the refined pleasures of life.'

This comment brings us to a fifth item in American prosperity, namely, increased leisure. Evidence of this appears not only in the shorter working week, but also in the astounding increase in the numbers who go to college.

Participation in the refined pleasures of life, we must remember, requires leisure. Leisure is a by-product of economic efficiency. And leisure is not a flashy thing.

Are the Poor Growing Poorer?

'THE rich are growing richer, and the poor are growing poorer.' For generations, this has been a favorite slogan of the soap-box orator. He has been at least half right. The rich *have* been growing richer.

The other half of the slogan is the subject of two exhaustive investigations, the results of which have been published in two large volumes; one by the National Bureau of Economic Research, the other by the Pollak Foundation for Economic Research. Both are non-profit-making enterprises, and their statistical work is as free from class prejudice as a cash register. The value of the two studies is further increased by the fact that they were wholly independent, and to some extent based on different sources of material.

The outstanding discovery of both studies is that the buying power of wages in the United States has increased, since 1914, fully 34 per cent.

Moreover, the share of the realized national income which labor received for its services *increased* from about 51 per cent in 1909 to about 57 per cent in 1928. On the other hand, the income of property owners (money and commodity income combined) *declined* from about 42 per cent of the total to about 37 per cent.

It is interesting to note that if wages and salaries gain at the same rate during the next twenty years, wages and salaries will make up about 64 per cent of the national income. That will be almost exactly twice as much as the money and commodity income of property owners.

There are, moreover, several times as many wage-earners as there were twenty years ago who, in addition to wages, receive income from property. The soap-box orator can still wave his hands and shout that the poor are growing poorer. But the facts are against him.

'Now, at This Time'

IN five years, according to Federal income tax returns, the number of people in the United States who receive incomes of over $100,000 increased 174 per cent. The total income of these people increased 214 per cent.

During these same five years, employment in factories fell off steadily. Machines crowded out men. New inventions took the place of old workers.

One result is that the workers who now hold their jobs produce more wealth than ever before; at least a third more than they produced before the War.

Another result is that, during these same five years, the number of homeless and jobless men applying for free shelter in the Municipal Lodging House in New York City steadily increased. The daily average in 1929 was higher than it was even in the major business depression of 1920.

Evidently, we know how to produce wealth.

Evidently, we have much to learn about distributing wealth.

It is not enough that the rich should grow richer and most of the poor should grow richer, too. Out of our abundance, we should find out how to meet the needs of the workers who are displaced by improved machinery. There should be no victims of progress!

Centuries ago, Paul wrote to the Corinthians: 'I mean not that other men should be eased, and ye burdened; but by an equality, that now, at this time, their abundance may be a supply for your wants.'

At last we are learning that most of the involuntary unemployment, and the poverty, anguish, and crime that go with it, can be abolished *now, at this time.*

After all, Paul *had* seen a great light.

'Let God Run It'

SAYS a member of the United States Senate: 'I would rather postpone a panic until the time when God brings it, than to have Hoover entrusted with this power and get the panic a year sooner. We had better let God run it, as in the past.'

That sounds stupid, doesn't it? Yet it is very much like the *laissez-faire* economics which used to be highly respected, and which is still soberly taught in many places.

In the past, to be sure, we did not call a major business depression an 'act of God.' We called it the result of natural law. 'In economics, as in physics,' we said, 'every action is followed by an opposite and equal reaction. The farther business moves forward in a period of expansion, the farther back it must slip when the reaction comes.'

That is, in fact, about what business suffered in the past. It happened, however, not as a result of 'natural law'; it came about largely as a result of financial methods deliberately devised by man.

Fortunately, methods devised by man can be improved by man. The ingenuity of man substituted money for barter. The ingenuity of man substituted the Federal Reserve System for a much poorer system. And the ingenuity of man can devise means of supplying a flow of money to consumers which, after providing for savings, will be approximately equal, at all times, to the flow of finished goods.

That means prosperity. A business depression caught in that sort of flow would throw up its hands and sink without a struggle.

No 'act of God' was responsible for the money panics we used to have. No 'act of God' is the cause of 'hard times.' Man made his own law of business depressions, and under that law he convicted himself. He is tired of serving his self-imposed sentence. He is intent on obtaining his economic pardon.

'Stop' and 'Go' Signs of the Zodiac

THROUGHOUT the summer months, when business is 'seasonally dull,' we wait for the months when business will be 'seasonally brisk.' Most of the business publications appear to assume that there is nothing for us to do *but* wait. At last September comes. Then all we have to do is to sit back and watch business get brisk.

If that is what everybody really thought, business would be about as brisk as a funeral procession. The approach of the autumnal equinox does not, in itself, open up blast furnaces or ring cash registers. The movements of the heavenly bodies do not move goods.

Business is better in the fall only if enough human beings *make* it better. Not a single transaction takes place until some man or woman decides to take a risk and spend money.

That is not a reassuring thought. It is much more comforting to blame Divine Providence for abnormal dullness in the markets. We are loath to blame the normal dullness of our own thinking. We need never do so, according to much of the economic teaching of the past. Perhaps that is one reason why we have regularly forecast seasonal weaknesses in the markets, and complacently accepted them when they came.

There are, to be sure, certain seasons when crops have to be harvested; and there are fluctuations in the goods volume of trade which have to do with the size of crops. But all the crop statistics put together do not reveal any convincing reason why trade, as a whole, *has* to be dull in August.

Some day we may discover that all 'seasonal slumps' in trade are largely the result of seasonal slumps in effort. Then we shall no longer look upon the signs of the Zodiac as though they were official 'Stop' and 'Go' signals for business.

'They That be for Us'

ELISHA, about to go into battle, sent his servant out to reconnoiter. The servant came back, his carburetor flooded with foreboding, and his fighting gear in reverse.

He had seen the enemy, and he was theirs.

Elisha, however, was unmoved. All he did in response to his servant's frantic report of the enemy was to begin to pray.

The servant doubted whether it would do any good to pray for extra chariots. Still, he listened respectfully. To his bewilderment, the Prophet had nothing at all to say about extra chariots. He prayed only that his servant's eyes might be opened.

The servant felt like retorting that his eyes were perfectly capable of seeing the enemy, and that was enough. Instead, something told him to look carefully around his *own* camp. He was amazed.

'Why,' he cried, 'they that be for us, are more than they that be against us!'

Elisha's prayer had been answered. Up to that time the servant had been too intent upon discovering the strength of the enemy. He had overlooked the strength of his own forces.

To-day many Servants of Elisha are abroad in the land. They are press agents for business depression. With shaking of heads, they describe the serried ranks of the enemy. 'What,' they ask, 'can we do against such as these?'

The answer is 'nothing' as long as we waste our time praying for more chariots — or more machines, or materials, or money, or men. 'Nothing' — as long as we cannot see that, when a business depression sets in, we have at hand all the productive facilities that we had when business was good — everything, in fact, except the nerve to use what we have.

Elisha's prayer is to the point. All we have to do is to open our eyes and take a look at the forces that await our command.

'The Fullness Thereof'

GIVE a man a roaring river to tame and he is so eager to tackle the job that his mouth waters. Show him a desert that went dry before Kansas and intended to stay dry, and he will criss-cross it with irrigation ditches, until it gives the impression of having been platted out with a waffle iron.

Introduce him to a fever-infested jungle between two oceans, and by the time he has said 'How do you do,' he will be building a canal. He re-vamps even California — which, we are told, God had specifically in mind when he declared His work was very good. In short, the earth, which man did *not* make, never daunts him. He can engineer his way around any obstacle it offers.

But over money, which he *did* make, he exercises only the sketchiest jurisdiction. When interest rates start running a temperature, or when factories close because money which ought to be on hand to move goods has checked out and gone to Palm Beach, the busy biped who engineers his way through mountains of solid rock, proceeds meekly to take his punishment.

Instead of setting matter-of-factly to work to engineer his way out of this jam by developing a technique to make money stop its antics, he folds his hands and intones mournfully: 'The Law of Supply and Demand giveth. The Law taketh away. Blest be the name of the Law.'

Truly, the burial service of hope; and one that never need be chanted.

The genius that controls currents can also control currency. Not, of course, by guesswork, but by means of accurate measurements.

Man seeks to control the earth. Surely he can exercise more than his present sketchy jurisdiction over the fullness thereof.

Turnips, Golden-Rod, and Dodos

THE man who first said, 'You can't get blood from a turnip,' was not a scientist. A scientist would have contented himself with the cautious statement: 'As far as we now know, no process has yet been discovered by which to extract blood from turnips'; implying, in his open-minded way, that any morning we might see the headline, 'Humble Turnip Gives Pint of Vital Fluid: Saves Life of Prominent Citizen.'

Silly? Not necessarily so. The blood-and-turnip tradition started only by chance. Its author, casting around for a picturesque phrase to denote impossibility, might have snorted: 'You can't get rubber out of golden-rod.' In that case, we should already have been deprived of a pet phrase, because you *can* get rubber from golden-rod. At least, Edison has announced that *he* can.

Science never yawns and calls it a day. It never indulges in vapid commonplaces about 'the usual amount' of waste and inefficiency. It accepts no new good as final. It accepts no old evil as necessary.

Business men are now taking on this open-minded attitude. They are checking up on their long-cherished opinions to see if these opinions are justified. They are becoming hesitant about mentioning things that 'can't be done.' They are developing willingness to admit that almost anything which will increase the happiness of humanity *can* be done.

Any one who still has a pet 'impossibility' would do well to chloroform it and have it stuffed. For now that science and business are hunting in pairs, it is likely to be shot to pieces anyway.

Even the 'Impossibility-of-Abolishing-Poverty' may some day be as extinct as the dodo.

'Painting the Clouds'

RADIO troubadours urge us to start 'painting the clouds with sunshine.' This poetic conception may be fraught with grand possibilities. But for those practical souls who don't know how to go about it, we suggest a substitute: 'Start painting the house with paint.'

Clouds, like peevish children, respond amazingly to a little ignoring. By the time you get your own renovating done, the clouds will have disappeared; and you will have one tangible asset — a freshly painted house.

Hope, which is the motif of the 'painting the clouds' composition, is a cheerful waiter. It expects that the sun will shine to-morrow. Faith is a busy doer. It goes ahead and acts as if the sun were shining to-day.

'Courage,' says Karle Baker, 'is Fear that has said its prayers.'

Faith is the Courage that goes right ahead and answers its own prayers.

There are no more conclusive words in the English language than 'evidence' and 'substance'! Paul, who knew his way about among words, uses them to define Faith. Faith acts. And activity is 'evidence.'

When the stock market collapses, sentimentalists cancel orders and console themselves with Hope. Fighters step out boldly into the arena and place larger orders — with Faith.

Alice Cary probably did not know a corn-hog ratio from a profit-and-loss statement, but there was an economic basis for her Faith: 'Get thy spindle and thy distaff ready; God will send the flax.'

Whenever business is better, it is better because States, cities, corporations, and individuals go ahead and make it better. The merely hopeful 'paint clouds with sunshine.' The faithful paint the house with paint.

The Spirit of the West

NEHEMIAH was the first man in recorded history with the Spirit of the West. His achievements in laying out a new city are summed up in the fourth chapter of Nehemiah:

'Now the city was large and great; but the people were few, and the houses were not yet builded.'

Nehemiah, as we understand it, did not erect on the walls of his city-to-be a huge electric sign: 'Watch Tacoma Grow.' He did well, however, with the meager advertising means at his disposal. When Sanballat urged him to stop building and come down from the city wall, he replied in words that may still be read, thanks to the Gideons, in any hotel room: 'I am doing a great work, so that I cannot come down.'

And when the people threatened him with calamity if he did not cease building, he said: 'Should such a man as I flee? I will not.'

So it has always been with the pioneers of the West. So it is to-day. Calamity howlers cannot get a hearing. The builders cannot be persuaded to stop their work.

The man with the true Spirit of the West is still a boy. He has found that we do not stop daring because we grow old: we grow old because we stop daring. Romance beckons to him. He is thrilled with the adventure. Nothing seems impossible. He cannot be persuaded to stop building and come down from his high wall.

Flood and fire, earthquake and panic, fruit flies and prophets of disaster — all find him smiling, confident, unafraid.

He sees his future large and great, although those who share his vision may be few, and the castles of his dreams are not yet builded.

Only a Fairy Tale

ONCE upon a time, there was a very large country, completely covered with gloom. Pessimism in the markets was so thick that you could cut it with a knife. But nobody did cut it. All the knives were used on those few bold prophets who dared to say a hopeful word about business.

For there was no hope. Business had gone to the dogs and would stay there. Nobody had any money to spend.

To know that the entire economic system had failed, however, was not enough for the 'Statistical Sadists.' They insisted on measuring the extent of the failure.

So an army of statisticians girded on their slide rules and drew up their calculating machines in battle array. Never before had any nation been so well equipped with moving averages and coefficient correlations. The problem was attacked simultaneously on many fronts. The offensive was brilliant.

When the smoke of battle cleared away, reports from the front revealed these facts:

In the depths of national gloom, the national income was about 50 per cent above the income of the previous decade.

At its worst, business was producing 30 per cent more, per capita, than business at its best in the previous generation.

Although business had gone to the dogs, it was still turning out enough wealth every day to maintain the highest standard of living ever reached by any people in the world.

Although nobody had any money, in no other year except one in the nation's history did consumers buy more goods.

The productive resources of the nation — men, machines, materials, money — were greater than ever before.

These were the findings of the army of statisticians. And so the gloom that settled over the nation was thicker than ever!

But this, of course, is only a fairy tale. No nation would act like that — really.

'What's the Use?'

A NATIVE of Bagdad, so goes an old fable, accosted the Plague as it was leaving the city. 'Why,' he demanded, bitterly, 'have you come here and killed ten thousand people?'

'You are mistaken,' laughed the Plague. 'I killed only one.'

'Who, then,' asked the man, 'killed all the rest?'

'Fear,' answered the Plague.

One of the worst of the Fears which stalk abroad to-day is 'What's the use.' Where native inability has slain one good impulse, this slinking assassin has slain his hundreds of thousands.

'What's the use' is so afraid it may be wasting some of its precious energy barking up the wrong tree, that it lies down and sobs itself to sleep at the foot of the right one.

'What's the use' is a mournful believer in the theory that business depressions must run their course; that nothing will be better until it gets worse.

'What's the use' has many aliases. In ecclesiastical robes, it is Resignation. In a smart business suit, it is Conservatism. In a hobo's outfit, it is Shiftlessness. But in any disguise it is Fear. Especially has it spread its chill over the subject of unemployment. If, it argues, you can't, by fretting, add a cubit to your stature, what's the use of worrying about adding men to your payroll? But the discovery that men out-of-wages are men out-of-the-price-of-goods, and that enough men out-of-the-price-of-goods mean business out-of-profits, has waked up many employers. They are finding ways of keeping men on the job more months of the year than they had supposed possible. Other employers are still blaming Economic Necessity for millions of slain hopes.

But the real villain is that snivelling purveyor of poison — 'What's the use?'

The Day of Judgment

NOT long ago, three persons in the Province of Saskatche-
wan made elaborate preparations for the End of the
World. They foresaw the approach of the Day of Judgment.

So the three prophets disposed of their farm lands and stock,
and pitched their tent high on a hill, overlooking the picturesque and soon-to-be-demolished town of Masefield. On their
camping ground they stored ten tons of flour, by way of special
preparation for the day of disaster.

Whereupon everybody except the prophets went about his
business as usual. For everybody knew that what the campers
on Masefield Hill *thought* about the date of disaster would not
greatly influence the movements of the heavenly bodies.

That is where the heavenly bodies have an advantage over
such mundane bodies as chambers of commerce and boards
of directors. For *their* movements really are influenced by
what men think — especially by what men think about the
approach of the end of good times. Even the most brilliant
stars in the firmament of business can be swayed from their
course by dismal forebodings.

In fact, *thinking* that disaster is at hand in the world of
business is the surest way of *bringing* disaster; not because of
any esoteric power in the thought itself, but because disastrous
thinking breeds disastrous acts. Business men who fear that
the buying of consumers will fall off usually so act as to *make*
it fall off.

If enough men forsook their usual pursuits, and camped out
on the top of the nearest hill, and prophesied the coming of
a business depression, the depression would come sure enough
— right on scheduled time — even if each of the prophets was
so wary as to take ten tons of flour with him.

'Give 'em Both Barrels'

A BREATHLESS boy thrust his head through the door of a house in the Ozark Mountains, in Arkansas.

'Hey, Doc,' he gasped, 'git up ter Hawkins' shack quick's you kin git. The gal's ailin'.'

'Doc' bent over the moaning girl. Ailin', indeed! A few minutes more and a ruptured appendix would put her beyond the reach of mortal ailments.

'I'm going to operate,' he said sharply to her father. 'You'll have to hold the lamp and ——'

'Cut her up, will ye?' snarled the frantic father. 'All right, go ahead an' cut up my gal, but her pappy ain't holdin' no lamp fer ye. He's holdin' a shotgun. Ef'n she lives, so do you. Ef'n she dies ——'

The crazed man glared at the Doctor. 'Sharpen yer knife, ye butcher, but don't let hit slip. *Don't let hit slip.*'

So in a mountain shack, by the light of the one kerosene lamp on the wall, the doctor set about the business of saving a life, with a shotgun held at his head.

The 'gal' lived. Then the Doctor sat down and for ten minutes spoke pure Ozark to her pappy and never used the same word twice.

There must be, up and down the land, many leaders of industry who would pay real money for that speech, and who would walk miles to clasp 'Doc' by the hand.

Business is ailin'. Many leaders of industry are operating under discouraging conditions, while those who should at least be holding lamps are holding shotguns. 'If business recovers,' they say, 'all well and good. If it doesn't — give 'em both barrels.'

What is a Luxury?

WE used to think that any business which dealt with the 'necessities' of life — food, clothing, housing — was for that reason on a firm foundation; and any business which dealt with 'luxuries' was trying to get a footing on shifting sands.

But mass production and mass distribution have made the 'luxury' of yesterday the 'necessity' of to-day. Example omnipresent, the automobile. The people of the United States now spend at least four billion dollars a year for pleasure motoring. For other 'luxuries' that did not exist a generation ago — motion pictures, phonographs, radios, airplanes — they now spend no less than three billion dollars.

These seven billions are what they have left over, after spending another seven billions for candy, chewing gum, tobacco, travel, night clubs, and other 'entertaining' that by no stretch of imagination can be called a 'necessity' — even if it can be called 'entertaining.'

Altogether, we now spend more for luxuries than our grandfathers spent for the three great staples: food, clothing, housing. We employ at least one fourth of our workers in making things which were unheard of at the beginning of this century. Many luxuries have become staples, and many staples have become producers' risks.

What can the old-line manufacturer do about it? He can complain of the extravagance of this age. Often he does complain, bitterly. Or he can stop trying to decide for other people what things are luxuries and what things are necessities, and produce the things they want — produce, also, things which they do not yet know they want.

New 'luxuries' produced by old industries; new industries produced by old communities. That is the way ahead.

Are Automobiles Luxuries?

CHRISTOPHER MORLEY'S *Candor* should have been entitled *An Ode to Bankers*. 'From time to time,' he says, 'I have laid my heart bare before you, and you did not care for it. So I must point out to you that it is my heart, not yours. It may be that my wrongness is dearer to me than your rightness.'

Once upon a time, the banks cut down the credit granted to automobile dealers, on the ground that automobiles were luxuries. That idea, of course, was nothing but an opinion of the bankers.

The people promptly bought more cars than ever, thus showing that they were not interested in the opinion of the bankers. Since that time, moreover, the people have increased their purchases of automobiles more rapidly than their purchases of anything else.

Evidently, it is useless for bankers, or merchants, or governments, or reformers to insist that certain products are necessities, and others, luxuries. The people settle that question for themselves. If they spend a billion dollars more for automobiles and a billion dollars less for other things, it is because they want automobiles more than they want the other things. To insist that automobiles are luxuries is to engage in academic discussion.

So with radio sets and cigarettes. So with silk stockings and fur coats. So with everything else. Bank 'rightness,' which is often wrong, cannot take the place of our own 'wrongness,' which is often right.

All of us, no doubt, can cultivate higher tastes. We can learn how to spend our money for the more durable satisfactions of life. We can *make* them necessities for us. And it will pay us well to do so. But that cannot be done through the control of bank credit.

Education is the only way.

199

Quantity Production of Quality

W HAT would happen to America,' asks a critic of mass production, 'if quality instead of quantity became the style?' This is merely a restatement of the great European myth, 'When quantity production comes in at the door, quality must go out through the window.'

Did the household slave who once toiled all day over one copper kettle turn out a better product than the mechanical slave which now presides over a hundred vats of Ivory soap?

Did Abe Lincoln make better fences with his split rails than we make by machinery to-day? Or did the rails merely represent more hard labor?

Mass production in America has all but banished the idea that nothing can be well done unless it is laboriously done. Machines not only make more goods than we can make by hand; as a rule, machines make better goods. Utility must be served. To the extent that machines meet the requirements of utility, men are released to consider the claims of beauty.

But do they? At least, the New England Council has held a series of 'Art in Industry' conferences. Industry, which used to have millions for utility, but not one cent for tribute to beauty, is getting line-and-color-conscious. Manufacturers know that beautiful advertisements pay. Why, they ask, shouldn't beautiful products pay?

Once American Industry becomes convinced that beauty pays, it will produce beauty. Our European critics will be the first to admit that. But Industry will not forsake mass production. It will produce quality goods in quantity.

'Suffer, Little Children'

WROTE Sarah Cleghorn:

'The golf links lie so near the mill,
That almost every day,
The laboring children can look out,
And see the men at play.'

If these children had time to look out of the windows, and had telescopic vision, they would see a million adults with plenty of time to play golf, but no chance to play. They are looking for jobs.

One million children who ought not to work, and are forced to work! One million adults who ought to work, and are forced to be idle!

Governor Roosevelt, of New York, made this blunt comment: 'If employing child labor is the only way to keep factories in this State, I say simply, from the bottom of my heart, that I would rather see the factories go.'

We are inclined to add, from the bottom of our hearts, 'Who wouldn't?'

This is one case where the bromide, 'There ought to be a law,' becomes (or ought to become) a stimulant to backward State legislatures.

What business needs, says *The Business Week*, is 'more sweat and less swagger.' But business also needs less sweat on the part of working children, and, in consequence, more justified swagger on the part of adults.

St. Peter, it is said, frowningly asked a new arrival at the Gate, 'Are you the man who employed little girls at six dollars a week?'

'I am not,' replied the applicant, indignantly. 'All I did was set fire to an orphan asylum and rob a blind man of his pennies.'

'Come in,' said St. Peter.

War and Long Division

IS it possible to master long division? This burning question was once solemnly debated in Roman treatises on mathematics. At that time long division seemed a tough problem. The toughness, however, was not in the problem; it was in the tools. Roman numerals were the real obstacle: they were unwieldy tools. Approached with Arabic numerals, long division is so meek that even children wrestle successfully with it.

Is it possible to abolish war? This problem also has nothing inherently difficult in it. The difficulty lies in finding the proper tools. We can abolish war with the mental tools of common sense, a conviction of its absurdity, and the will-to-progress. We cannot abolish it with mental tools dulled and warped by fear and suspicion.

We admit that war is uneconomic. We admit that it is unsocial. We are now venturing a hopeful foot into the coldly matter-of-fact question, 'Is it necessary?' Presently, we shall be prepared to plunge in all over and admit that it is not at all necessary.

That the great nations of the world would ever gather to make peace permanent once seemed a hope that overstepped 'the narrow bourne of likelihood.' But the likelihood of permanent peace is every day enlarging its borders.

One of our great-grandsons may look up from his pet editorial page some evening and chuckle: 'Listen to this: Can we abolish war? That question was seriously debated by our forefathers.'

And great-granddaughter-in-law will murmur indulgently: 'As if there ever was any sense in their crazy wars!'

Anyway, the pert young Future Generation will have to credit us with one accomplishment: We can now mention 'Disarmament' without being afraid the world will grow a set of teeth and bite us.

World Peace, Preferred

THROUGH the Kellogg Pact, the nations have outlawed war; a decisive victory — gained after ten thousand years of struggling. During all these centuries, the Captains and the Kings have insisted that fighting was inevitable. So, instead of trying to abolish war, they have tried to outdo each other in getting ready for war — thus helping to bring on war. But at last mankind has renounced the whole heinous business, poison-gas and all.

Now the time has come for renouncing the poison-gas practices which choke the industrial life of nations — practices which lead to war.

Here, again, the Captains and the Kings stand in the way. They hold that economic warfare between nations is inevitable. They insist that some nations must have closed mines, abandoned factories, idle men, and starving children, in order that other nations may prosper. So every nation tries to outdo every other nation in preparing for such calamities — thus helping to bring them on.

There is hope, however, in the fact that competition for markets is becoming less a rivalry of nations, and more a rivalry of corporations, owned by the people of many nations. In the automobile industry, for example, the chief struggle is between two great corporations, both born in the United States, both internationally owned. All over the world, Ford plants have been organized. In competition, General Motors has set up assembling units in twenty-four world markets. As a result, every American stockholder throws in his fortunes with stockholders from Buenos Aires to Bombay. Thus, the very thing which made for peace among our forty-eight States is a growing force for peace among forty-eight nations. Each nation is investing more and more heavily in 'World Peace, Preferred.'

A World Holiday

THERE are those who would have us abolish all national holidays because in their view nationalism is too narrow. They maintain that national holidays deepen devotion to country at the expense of the larger devotion to humanity. There are others who seek to abolish religious holidays. They would have us cherish the aspirations which draw men of all faiths together, rather than the differences which keep men apart.

Most of us believe, however, that devotion to country and to church do not necessarily prevent larger enthusiasms. We would not abolish what holidays we have, but liberalize them.

We would go a long step further. We would establish a World Holiday. Unhappily, not one of the hundreds of holidays which are now celebrated can ever become a World Holiday. Even Christmas would not do for three fourths of the world's population. In the past, no day has given the peoples of all nations common cause for rejoicing.

Now there is such a day — August 27 — the day which marks the ratification of the World Peace Pact. No other day in history is pregnant with such good for all mankind.

Many of our holidays had their origin in conflicts which were born of misunderstanding, greed, hatred, and r-.₋nge. Many of our holidays are celebrated, in part, so as to perpetuate misunderstanding, greed, hatred, and revenge.

Let us make August 27 a holiday on which travelers the world over, under every flag, will get together to strengthen their unity of purpose and rejoice in common aspirations.

Every year more than 300,000 travelers from the United States go to Europe. More are there in August than in any other month. Think what it would mean, as a permanent force for world peace, for them to unite, once a year, with the citizens of all nations in celebration of the renunciation of war!

Let the Buyer Rejoice!

MY son,' began the father, 'I have taught you the code of Family Life: loyalty, consideration, service, generosity. These precepts you have practiced from your childhood.

'But now,' he went on, gravely, 'you are about to assume the responsibilities of a man. You are going into business. In order to succeed, you must reverse every precept that I have taught you. Remember that business is business. Keep in mind the grand old precept, "Caveat Emptor," meaning "Let the buyer worry." Charge all the traffic will bear. Never consider any one's interests but your own. If you observe these principles, success will crown your efforts. And what is more, you'll be a business man, my son!'

The only exaggerated feature of this conversation is that it never occurred. No such preparation was offered the poor lad of a generation ago. He was left to find out the rules of business for himself.

But were such rules *ever* needed in business? Apparently not; for business itself is fast repudiating them, and is finding itself immeasurably the richer.

Standards of living are constantly becoming higher. So are standards of making a living. It is no longer considered necessary to take a degree in banditry in order to be a success in business. There is more and more competition among producers to give the most value for the least money. 'Charge as much as the traffic will bear' is discarded as bad ethics and bad business.

The modern business man is free to revert to his boyhood ideals without a guilty feeling that he is short-changing his heirs. The former Dr. Jekyll of business and the Mr. Hyde of family life are well on their way toward a reunion.

Let the buyer rejoice!

Who Can Afford to be Sick?

YOU and I, says Walter Hamilton, have learned the knack of buying bread and shoes and houses and bonds. Not so with medical care. The market for that is unique. The demand is for a necessity; failure in supply often means death; yet the patient who buys medical care in the open market runs serious risks.

Usually he does not know what he wants. How *can* he know? And even when he does know, he cannot tell when he finds it. 'If, on the other hand, he wants coffee, candy, or cigars; if his heart yearns for dancing, preaching, or faking, he gets just about what he asks for.' But medical service does not come in standardized packages. There is no test of worth which the buyer can apply. As a result, medical service is now bought with little knowledge of its quality.

Often, too, with little knowledge of its price. The patient commits himself to an unknown course, in which one bill may merely breed others. The price does not behave the way prices behave in textbooks on economics.

The physician also has his troubles. He does not collect a large part of his bills; and he usually complains that he does not receive an income commensurate with his long and costly preparation.

Meantime, most of the buyers in his care complain that they cannot afford it. And they cannot.

What shall we do about it? First, we ought to know the facts. Soon we shall; for the Committee on the Cost of Medical Care is engaged in five years of research in this field.

It is commonly said that the best medical care is within reach of only the very rich and the very poor. When it is within the reach of those of us who are neither rich nor poor, we can afford to be sick more. Thus relieved, we shall probably be sick less.

Who Goes to the Dentist ?

WHAT is the use of giving the workers more money?' asks one of our critics. 'They will merely spend it on more cosmetics, candy, and chewing gum. No doubt they *do* need more dental care, but the reason they do not get it is not lack of money.'

We have two direct answers to that criticism. Dr. Michael M. Davis, analyzing the expenditures of 1226 working-class families, finds that in the course of one full year, 61 per cent of these families spent nothing whatever for dental care.

Was there any relation between the family income and the care of the teeth? There certainly was. *Three fourths* of the families which had only $1200 a year, spent nothing for dental care; while only *one fourth* of the families with over $2500 a year spent nothing. Furthermore, only two per cent of the lower income families spent $30 a year for the services of dentists; whereas 20 per cent of the upper income families spent $30 a year. The trouble, evidently, is not mainly lack of intelligence in spending money, but mainly lack of money.

In further proof of this fact, Professor Jessica B. Piexotto cites the expenditures of 96 faculty families at the University of California. All these families, undoubtedly, were aware of the importance of dental care. Yet here, again, the amount of dental care received varied directly with the salaries received.

In the United States there is approximately one dentist to every 1800 persons. A single dentist to-day, however, cannot render adequate service to more than 500 persons. So about 70 per cent of the needed dental services are not rendered at all.

But, happily, the income of wage-earners has been increasing. Happily, too, there is every means at hand for making further increases. With these increases will come many things besides cosmetics, candy, and chewing gum. Notable among the gains will be better care of teeth.

'Back to Normal'

MANY persons are urging us to go 'Back to Normal.' Where is this place, and what shall we do when we get there? Shall we scrap our new Ford car and go back to the delights of a horse and buggy? Or will it be all right to have a Ford car, provided it is the old Model T? We are not sure. The press agents for this idyllic place do not say. They are enthusiastic but vague.

Some persons insist that the whole advertising campaign is a fraud. They say that you no sooner reach the promised land, and get ready to unpack your bag and enjoy yourself, than somebody proves that the place is somewhere else.

To tell the truth, we begin to suspect that there isn't any such place as 'Normal.' Even the 'Computed Normal,' as charted by business statisticians in this country, is always above and beyond the heights of the previous year.

The idea of 'Normal' as a safe place of refuge is an old one. It was urged upon Columbus by his sailors. They mutinied because they were sick and tired of permanent waves, and wanted to turn around and go 'Back to Normal.'

Even among the adventurous souls who scrambled out on Plymouth Rock, there were some who wanted to go 'Back to Normal,' where they could be beheaded in the good old-fashioned way, by a dignified executioner, instead of by an impulsive red Indian. Even among the pioneers who dragged their covered wagons over the Rockies, there were those who urged the leaders to go 'Back to Normal.'

But the leaders refused to go back.

So do the American people always refuse to go back. You can sell them the idea of going forward to almost anything — television, air travel, robots, mechanical translators, frosted foods, dial 'phones, even the abolition of poverty.

But you can't sell them the idea of going back.

Index

Index

Accidents, 160

Advertisers, fable of the, 149

Advertising, 56

Alcott, Amos B., cited, 25

Alice-in-Wonderland economics, 23

American Federation of Labor, cited, 125, 147

American Radiator Company, cited, 148

American Telephone and Telegraph Company, cited, 157

Assets, hidden, 144

Automatic-production-consumption theory, 5, 82

Automobile, a luxury, 199; factor in prosperity, 120

'B. and O. plan,' cited, 154

Baker, Karle, cited, 192

Balance of trade, 92, 95

Bank Catechism, cited, 92

Barter, why not trade by, 27

Blood-letting doctors, 99

Boulder Dam, 138

Bowers, Edison L., cited, 160

Brookhart, Smith W., cited, 112

Budgeting, benefits of, 175

Business, and government, 130–44; and stock speculation, 72; ideals of, 205; new methods of financing, 71; stimulated by disasters, 122; suffers if consumers lack money, 74–77; sunshine cure for, 78. *See also* Depression and Public works

Business Week, cited, 123, 201

Cameron, Lieut., cited, 27

Capital, conflict between labor and, 57, 158, 159; often works for nothing, 51

Capitalism, delivers the goods, 44; responsible for high standard of living, 57, 156

Carlyle, Thomas, cited, 10

Cary, Alice, cited, 192

Cheap labor, plenty of, 107

Chesterton, G. K., cited, 152

Chevrolet Motor Company, cited, 152

Child labor, 201

Chinese view of business, 21

Chores *vs.* charity, 112

Circulating medium, 121

Cleghorn, Sarah, cited, 201

Collective bargaining, 159

Committee on the Cost of Medical Care, cited, 206

Communist Manifesto, cited, 45

Communists, 103, 134

Consumption, not automatically financed by production, 5, 82; regulates production, 81

Coolidge, Calvin, cited, 125

Corporation aid in averting 'hard times,' 148–57, 172

Cows, used for money, 28

Davis, Michael M., cited, 207

Deflation, worse than inflation, 32

Dennison Manufacturing Company, cited, 154

Dental care, 207

Depression, bred by prosperity, 3; marked by general overproduction, 79; not an 'act of God,' 187, 196; not inevitable, 123, 124, 188–95

Detroit City Council, cited, 110

Dilemma of thrift, 173

Doctors of despair, 123, 147

Douglas, Paul H., cited, 98, 181, 182, 183

Economic illiterates, 7

Economic laws, applied internationally, 95; not policemen, 67

Economics, corner-store, 91; not an exact science, 180; of original sin, 123; puss-in-the-corner, 110. *See also* Science

Edison, Thomas A., cited, 24, 42, 191

Edison-Ford commodity money, 37

Elastic work day, 151

Elisha, cited, 88, 189

Emerson, Ralph Waldo, cited, 25

Employment exchanges, need for, 114, 146

Erskine, A. R., cited, 108

Index

212

Index

Index

Temple, Sir William, cited, 107
Thoreau, Henry D., cited, 46
Thrift, 166–75
Townsend, Rev. Joseph, cited, 107
Travelers, Insurance Company, cited, 160
Tucker, Josiah, cited, 107
Twain, Mark, cited, 133

Unemployment, and child labor, 201; and communism, 103; and doles, 112; and shorter hours, 90; conference on, cited, 114, 125; Federal census of, 118; helped by spending, 169, 170, 172, 173, 174; in Detroit, 110; problem of, 5, 6, 9–14, 74, 102, 111, 113, 114, 126, 146, 165, 195; technological, 3, 4. *See also* Public works and Wagner bills

United States Employment Service, 146

Wage-earners, gains of. *See Real Wages*
Wages, fixing of, 158, 159; higher, 89, 97, 98, 99, 100, 101, 106, 107
Wagner bills, cited, 135, 141, 143, 147
Want and wants, 18
War, and international investments, 203; and tariffs, 92; next, 80; production during, 8
Wealth of nations, 34
Webb, Sidney and Beatrice, cited, 44
Western Electric Company, cited, 162
Wood, Charles G., cited, 103
World holiday, 204

Yale Review, cited, 171